P9-ARX-013

American English

AMERICAN ENGLISH

SECOND EDITION

ALBERT H. MARCKWARDT

Revised by

J. L. DILLARD

New York • Oxford
OXFORD UNIVERSITY PRESS
1980

The English Language Teaching Department
Oxford University Press, New York

Manager: Marilyn Rosenthal, Ph.D.
Editor: Laurie Likoff, M.A.
Educational Specialist: Connie Attanasio, M.A.

Library of Congress Cataloging in Publication Data
Marckwardt, Albert Henry, 1903–1975.
American English.
Bibliography: p.   Includes index.
1. English language in the United States.
2. English language—History. I. Dillard, Joey Lee,
1924–   II. Title.
PE2808.M3   1980   420′.973   79-27599
ISBN 0-19-502600-4   ISBN 0-19-502609-8 pbk.

Contents

Acknowledgments

Gratitude is hereby expressed to Maybelle Marckwardt, who graciously made available to me the notes toward a revision of this book which her late husband had assembled.

Margie I. Dillard read the manuscript, having listened to me talk endlessly about it, and suggested many changes and improvements.

Emanuel Drechsel and H. F. Gregory helped me with the linguistic and onomastic materials on American Indians. None of these is responsible for any mistakes contained herein, which are completely my own.

Preface

When Professor Marckwardt first wrote this general treatment of *American English* in 1958, the state of linguistic knowledge—particularly concerning American English—was greatly different from what it is today. Within the field of linguistics, Noam Chomsky's study of *Syntactic Structures* (1957) had hardly had time to sound its first challenge to the then dominant structuralist position. Today, the transformationalist position has, to a large extent, replaced the structuralist position, and it is difficult to remember how it was once considered "scientific" to segment and classify spoken sentences in a given language.

At the time of Marckwardt's writing, the primary research project on American English was the *Linguistic Atlas* of the United States and Canada—a project with which Marckwardt had some connections. It is not surprising, then, that his presentation of dialect diversity and of change came primarily in terms of geographic variation and geographic spread.

Chief among the predecessors to whom Marckwardt gave credit for developing his approach were H. L. Mencken, whose *The American Language* (1919) gave an emphasis to foreign-language immigrant groups hardly accorded before or since, and G. P. Krapp's *The English Language in America* (1925), which looked primarily to the native speakers of English who came from Great Britain as the source of American English.

Marckwardt also cited excellent studies of special topics, rang- ing all the way from that of George R. Stewart on place names to Mamie Meredith's on the nomenclature of fences. He expressed an obligation to the *Oxford English Dictionary,* the *Dictionary of American English,* and the *Dictionary of Americanisms,* as well as to the splendid service rendered by the journal *American Speech.* He did not forget to pay a particular tribute to his linguistic col- leagues at the University of Michigan, particularly Charles C. Fries and Hans Kurath.

Although these are names that still must be reckoned with, the intervening twenty years have produced new leaders, a different orientation, and greatly increased knowledge about ethnic dialects. Still to come were the sociolinguistic projects of the 1960's, espe- cially William Labov's *Social Stratification of English in New York City* (1965), and the formal studies of variation (including inherent variability, even in the language of one speaker) that resulted from that approach. Historical researchers like William A. Stewart, oriented toward documentation as much as or more than internal reconstruction, began to point out both the early use of Pidgin English and the social (especially ethnic) factors in twen- tieth-century American dialects. Black English, perhaps the most widely researched and discussed dialect of the 1960's and 1970's, had barely received any attention at the time of Professor Marck- wardt's writing. My own research, reported especially in *Black English* (1972), and *All-American English* (1975), has suggested an importance for Pidgin English and other special contact varie- ties not dreamed of in the late 1950's. The fruits of this new research have been incorporated into the present edition.

While my primary contribution has been the revision of this book in line with current linguistic research, I have also made a great effort to retain Professor Marckwardt's viewpoint, when expressed, within this framework. The book remains non-technical, as before, and in most respects, I hope, does not depart much from the spirit of Professor Marckwardt's work.

Natchitoches, Louisiana   J. L. D.
June, 1980

American English

1

The English Language in America

How many people in the world speak English as a first or native language? Exact information on this point is not available, but 300 million, on four continents, would be a conservative estimate. Of these, close to 200 million live in the United States, about 50 million in the United Kingdom, and 100 to 150 million in what were formerly British dominions and colonial possessions. It is even more difficult to arrive at a figure representing those who speak English as a second or auxiliary language. Here the guesses range from 500 million to 700 million. A reasonably conservative conclusion would thus place the total number of speakers of English between 800 and 900 million, nearly one-fourth of the world's population.

If one thinks solely in terms of total numbers of speakers, it must be conceded that some authorities have placed Chinese, the various Indic languages, and Russian ahead of English. Both Chinese and Indic, however, are terms covering a large number of mutually unintelligible dialects, and though the numbers of speakers may seem impressive, communication within these languages is much more restricted than in English. Total numbers, moreover, constitute but one aspect of the matter. The factor of geographic distribution is equally, perhaps even more, significant. English is spoken as a first or native language on at least four continents of the world; Russian on two, Chinese and Indic languages on one. English is, without question, the closest approximation to a world language available today, especially if one includes Pidgin English varieties like that of New Guinea (Tok Pisin).

It is generally understood that no two persons ever have an identical command of their common language. Certainly they do not have the same vocabulary. There are at least minor differences in pronunciation; in fact, the same individual will not pronounce his vowels and consonants in absolutely identical patterns each time he speaks. Everyone possesses, in addition, certain individual traits of (surface) grammatical form and syntactical order, constituting that peculiar and personal quality of language termed *style*. No two people are identical, so no two styles of speech are the same. When one considers the differences between any two speakers of a language, the potential for linguistic diversity resident in a language spoken by almost a billion people truly staggers the imagination. Despite this diversity, most modern linguists agree that there is a common underlying (deep) structure present in the varieties of any one language, although they may differ as to how that deep structure is represented.

The peculiar use of language characteristic of any one person depends largely upon his peer relationships, particularly those that existed during the language-acquiring and language-forming years. Home environment, education, occupation, and recreational habits, as well as the political, social, and religious institutions in which a person participates all share in determining which people one identifies with and therefore speaks most like. It is reasonable to assume that speakers with a similar environmental background will be more alike in their language, as in other modes of behavior, than those hailing from widely disparate surroundings. Of the total population of English speakers, the 200 million who live in the United States have a number of formal and institutional factors in common. This is also true of the 50 million or so British speakers of English who also share a common environment. Looking at such factors as political, economic, and monetary systems, as well as social organization, one would expect to find certain characteristic differences between British and American English. When, however, we consider the vast influence of the so-called counter-culture on both British and American teenagers of the 1960's and 1970's, we might expect terms like *grass* (marijuana), *split* (leave), and *freak out* (be extremely shocked or impressed), to be better known to that age group without regard to which side of the Atlantic they live on.

A certain number of terms are, nonetheless, divided by the ocean, so that few native Americans who have not lived in England for any great length of time would be able to explain the meaning of *spanner, gearbox, leat, lasher,* or *switchback.* And even if they could understand such terms as *petrol, oddments, bus caravan,* or *superannuation scheme,* they would not normally employ them. Nor is this arbitrary collection of Britishisms the result of any extensive search. Words such as these may be found in any daily newspaper published in England; they are a part of the ordinary vocabulary of every speaker of British English. Conversely, then, those in the United States must also be prepared to recognize that *monkey wrench, transmission, roller coaster, gasoline, leftovers, house trailer,* and *retirement plan* would sound quite as strange and unusual to the average speaker of British English. Americans who read the comic strip "Andy Capp" know the term *telly,* and Britishers exposed to American popular culture from various sources know *TV;* but neither group would feel natural using the other's term.

There are, of course, constant reminders that these two great divisions of English-speaking people do not always understand each other without special effort. American forces stationed in England during World War II were provided with little booklets indicating some of the outstanding differences between British and American customs and language, and less formal instructions for travelers have been more or less standard items for years. Such novels and plays as *Main Street* and *Brother Rat* were originally supplied with glossaries for the British trade. In British novels of the past, like Gilbert Frankau's *The Royal Regiment,* statements such as the following often reflected the author's conception of the differences between the two varieties of the English language:

> "I'm sorry," she said in her turn; and relapsing into a rare Americanism, "but that's all there is to it."

> Camilla refused a taxi, saying, "The shop's only just around the corner." He chafed her for the Americanism.

Today, terms like *relapsing* and *chafed* might, in view of the increased prestige of American English, no longer be likely to occur in such a novel.

A few decades ago, Lion Feuchtwanger's novel *The Oppermans* was translated from the German, first by an Englishman and then by an American. A comparison of the two versions, made by Edmund E. Miller, brings out some interesting differences between American and British vocabulary. The following are some of the variant translations of the same German word or expression:

American	British
subway (train)	underground (train)
furniture store	furnishing store
newspaper clipping	newspaper cutting
That's tough!	Oh crumbs!
lousy slob	great impudent oaf
from the ground up	to the last detail
elevator	lift
to have the jitters	to get icebergs down your back
It was nearly six o'clock.	It was getting on for six o'clock.
What did he have to do today?	What had he got to do today?

While many of these expressions are no longer current today, they do point up the long-standing differences between British and

American English. A sign is supposed to have appeared in a Paris shop window, prior to the great influx of American tourists following World War II, which read ENGLISH SPOKEN—AMERICAN UNDERSTOOD. Europeans once familiar primarily with British English have, in the last decades, grown accustomed to the American idiom.

It is apparent then that American English does possess certain qualities peculiar to itself. On more linguistic grounds, the degree of autochthony which may be ascribed to it has been a matter of some difference of opinion and is strikingly reflected in the titles of two historically influential books on the subject. Shortly after the close of the First World War, H. L. Mencken, who, as co-editor of the magazine *Smart Set,* was then the literary bad boy of the United States, assumed the role of philologist and surprised the world of letters with his book *The American Language.* Six years later, Professor George Philip Krapp of Columbia University published a two-volume work on the same subject, which he called *The English Language in America.*

The difference in these two titles reflects a thoroughgoing difference in attitude toward the material under consideration. Mencken at that time, with his attention fixed on the spoken language, felt that "the American form of the English language was plainly departing from the parent stem, and it seemed likely that the differences between American and English would go on increasing." 'This,' he said, 'was what I argued in my first three editions.' " Krapp, more concerned with the written, in fact the formal literary language, took the opposite point of view, insisting that "historical and comparative study brings American English in closer relation to the central tradition of the English language than is commonly supposed to exist."

These differing viewpoints were far from equally received. Mencken's thesis, although much more accessible to the layman, did not appeal to the academic world. The language historians tended to follow Krapp. Works like Thomas Pyles's *Words and Ways in American English* (1954), which avowedly took a lot of data from Mencken, essentially disregarded Mencken's thesis of the language status of American English. Few writers have since attempted either to match Mencken's iconoclasm or to defend his thesis.

To apply, as Mencken did, the term *language* to the American variety of English implies a much greater degree of mutual unintelligibility between it and British English than there actually is. A Yorkshireman and an Alabaman will not understand each other easily and without some effort, but they will understand one another. Using whatever skills of wider communication each has acquired, virtually any American speaker can establish spoken communication with virtually any British speaker.

If Mencken's title was too extreme, Krapp's scarcely suggested enough. If English in this country has maintained the "central tradition of the English language" (with the exceptions of the Creole language, Gullah, and arguably, Hawaiian Creole English and the Black English vernacular), it has at the same time reflected with great fidelity those facets of cultural history and development which are peculiar to our people and our milieu. *American English,* the title of the present work, suggests precisely this. The term *English* denies the implication of a separate language. At the same time, the modifier *American* is intended to indicate more than the mere transplanting of a vernacular to a new soil, but rather to suggest its new growth as a somewhat changed and wholly indigenous organism. It should never be forgotten, moreover, that a title is merely a label, and subject to all the limitations of labeling. If dialect research of the last four decades has taught us anything, it is that every sub-group of the population has its own linguistic repertoire, frequently overlapping with that of other groups but never being completely identical.

Certain characteristic vocabulary differences between British and American English—considered without specific reference to the sub-group repertories indicated above—have already been mentioned. That there are also differences in pronunciation is so obvious as to require no demonstration. Close scrutiny will also reveal some differences in grammatical structure, superficial in most cases but becoming increasingly deeper as we consider some of the sub-groups. The Black English vernacular, for example, has recently been shown to have preverbal *been* (He *been* ate de chicken; you *been* know dat) not directly paralleled elsewhere except in Pidgin and Creole varieties from West Africa, New Guinea, the West Indies, and other primarily insular and coastal areas around the world. To some extent, then, the immense potential of variation in a language with more than 800 million speakers is now being realized.

There are, despite the partly mythical concept of the Melting Pot, many heterogeneous aspects to American culture. Blacks, Jews, Chicanos, and other ethnic groups maintain some internal uniformity although geographically dispersed in the United States. Occupational, religious, recreational, and other social groups have their own interests and in some sense their own "language." Even mainstream culture has regional manifestations in areas like New England, the Old South, the Middle West, the Rocky Mountain and Great Plains area, the Southwest, and the Far West.

Diverse linguistic and cultural groups in different regional contact patterns appear to have given a certain distinctiveness to regional dialects. Speakers from New England and the Coastal South can usually be recognized by the conglomerate profiles of features in their speech, although, outside of vocabulary items, hardly a single individual feature is peculiar to no other region. Other sections also have recognizable patterns of variation.

The relationship between language, its vocabulary and structure, and the background and environment of the individual speaker (or his sub-group) has already been suggested. We may approach this same relationship in a somewhat broader fashion by saying that language is a social tool or a social organism. As such it is the product of the society which employs it, and as it is employed it is engaged in a continual process of re-creation. If this is the case, we may reasonably expect a language to reflect the culture, the folkways, and the characteristic psychology of the people who use it.

Operating from the kind of profile approach which finds a perceptible difference between American English and its British counterpart, we come to the question, "How does this variety (or these varieties) of American English reflect those facets of cultural history, institutional development, and physical environment which are peculiar to English-speaking groups on the North American continent and which are not shared with speakers of English elsewhere on the globe?" In short, how does American English reflect the American tradition and the American character? And further, what language processes have operated to produce such differences between British and American varieties, and how have they operated? It is with these particular questions that the ensuing chapters of this book will be concerned.

2

The Language
of the Colonists

In considering the history and development of American English we must remember that the courageous people who ventured westward into the unknown with Captain John Smith, or on board the *Mayflower,* as well as those who followed them later in the seventeenth century, were speaking and writing the language varieties of their own day. We must look then at the varieties of English which are attested from that period, whether in England or (as special contact varieties) abroad. It has always seemed safe to conclude that the linguistic processes which operated to produce the differences between today's American and British English must either have taken place in American English after the colonists settled on this continent, or have developed in British English after the emigrants left their homeland. There is, however, the third possibility that there may have been changes in both divisions of the language after the original period of settlement. In fact, all the documentation currently available supports this last alternative. Original identity and subsequent change have always been the working assumption in the reconstruction of two language branches from one trunk. It now appears, however, that we

IMPORTANT DATES IN THE SETTLEMENT OF AMERICA AND ENGLISH LITERARY HISTORY

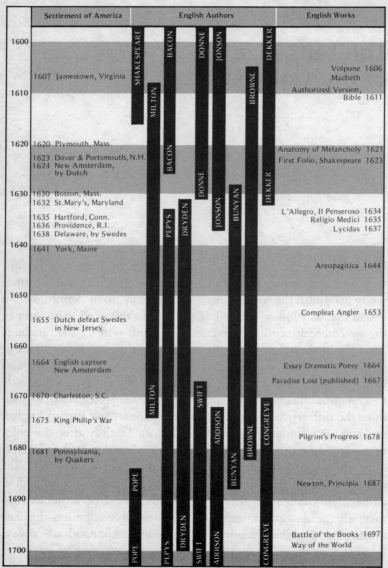

	Settlement of America	English Authors	English Works
1600		SHAKESPEARE · BACON · DONNE · JONSON · DEKKER	
	1607 Jamestown, Virginia		Volpone 1606 Macbeth
1610		MILTON · BROWNE	Authorized Version, Bible 1611
1620	1620 Plymouth, Mass.		
	1623 Dover & Portsmouth, N.H.	BACON	Anatomy of Melancholy 1621 First Folio, Shakespeare 1623
	1624 New Amsterdam, by Dutch	DONNE	
1630	1630 Boston, Mass.		
	1632 St. Mary's, Maryland		
	1635 Hartford, Conn.	PEPYS · DRYDEN · JONSON · BUNYAN · DEKKER	L'Allegro, Il Penseroso 1634
	1636 Providence, R.I.		Religio Medici 1635
	1638 Delaware, by Swedes		Lycidas 1637
1640	1641 York, Maine		
			Areopagitica 1644
1650			
	1655 Dutch defeat Swedes in New Jersey		Compleat Angler 1653
1660			
	1664 English capture New Amsterdam		Essay Dramatic Poesy 1664
		SWIFT	Paradise Lost (published) 1667
1670	1670 Charleston, S.C.	MILTON	
	1675 King Philip's War	ADDISON · BROWNE · CONGREVE	
1680	1681 Pennsylvania, by Quakers		Pilgrim's Progress 1678
		POPE · BUNYAN	Newton, Principia 1687
1690			
		PEPYS · DRYDEN · SWIFT · ADDISON · CONGREVE	Battle of the Books 1697 Way of the World
1700		POPE	

must have some idea of whatever diversity there may have been within the original source itself.

Our first concern, therefore, is with the kinds of English available to John Smith's Virginians, George Calvert's Marylanders, the Plymouth Fathers, the Bostonians of the Massachusetts Bay Colony, Roger Williams' Rhode Islanders, and William Penn's Quakers. We must also consider the English available to the West African slaves that were imported to the New World to provide manual labor; the language used by the American Indians in contact with Englishmen; and the many immigrant groups who spoke European languages other than English. Recent linguistic research has emphasized the use of Pidgin English, particularly among the non-English groups. What was the nature of those special contact languages? And what was the state of the English language at the time the colonizers left the shores of their native England? These are the two most important questions we have to consider.

The answer to the second entails making a comparison between the memorable dates of our early colonial history and those pertinent to the English literary scene throughout the seventeenth century. In this connection the tabulation on the preceding page may prove helpful. It shows, for example, that Ben Jonson was at the height of his career and that William Shakespeare was still writing when Jamestown was settled. Plymouth Colony was founded less than a decade after the completion of that great influence on English style, the Authorized Version of the Bible.

John Dryden, who is often called the father of modern literary prose, was born after the settlement of the second colony in New England. His *Essay of Dramatic Poesy* was not written until the capture of New York by the English, nor were the essays of Abraham Cowley, which are equally modern in style and temper. The publication date of *Paradise Lost* is somewhat later, and that of *Pilgrim's Progress* actually follows King Philip's War in point of time. These are mentioned in particular because the last two works are often thought of as indicative of the same kind of dissent against the Anglican Church as that which was reflected in the colonial settlement, particularly in the north. Yet Massachusetts, Connecticut, and Rhode Island were all established and flourishing by the time these books appeared. Even such late prose representative of Elizabethan exuberance, complication, and to some extent lack of discipline as Robert Burton's *Anatomy of Melancholy* and Thomas Browne's *Religio Medici* postdate the establishment of the early New England settlements.

Known to seafaring men and to at least some of the early settlers were, however, contact language expedients which even involved the use of a variety of Portuguese. Richard Hakluyt's *Voyages* tells us more than all the poets of the language could about those contact varieties. It may be that Shakespeare's *The Tempest* describes what stay-at-home Englishmen fantasized to be in the West Indies, but the realities encountered by the Elizabethan *sea dogs* were much different. "Broken English" of the type that William Bradford's men heard at Plymouth from "Squanto" (Tisquantum) was in evidence, especially among the new populations of non-European provenance. There proved to be no Calibans on the islands or the coasts of the New World, but there was linguistic diversity such as the most daring poet might never have envisaged. The West African slaves, coming from multilingual groups partly traceable to the intentional mixing of the slave ship cargoes, spoke a Pidgin English which their masters could well learn to understand but at which they frequently marveled. Sheridan's *The Rivals* gives us, in the character of Mrs. Malaprop, one version of what the language could be like when re-imported to England from the Indies. "Malapropism" is, of course, a term available to the satirist, who does not share the responsibility of cultural and linguistic relativism which the historical linguist must always assume.

Insofar as the more home-grown varieties of English relevant to the present consideration are concerned, it can be pointed out that the emigrés who accompanied Smith and Bradford had learned their native language long before the years 1607 and 1620 respectively. Many of them were mature; some were old. Even a man of forty on the Jamestown expedition would presumably have learned to speak English about 1570. John Rolfe, who as future husband of Pocahontas may symbolize the extensive contacts of all kinds with the Indians, probably acquired his native tongue in 1587. A young man of twenty-one, John Alden for example, in the Mayflower company must have learned English at the height of Shakespeare's career; Miles Standish, when Shakespeare was beginning to write. In short, the earliest English colonists in the New World spoke, among themselves, Elizabethan English, the language of Shakespeare, Lyly, Marlowe, Lodge, and Green. The measurably different English of Dryden, Defoe, and Bunyan was still to develop in the mother country. Some of the observable changes between the former and the latter group presumably affected American English little, or not at all. This is an important and necessary point for our understanding of some of the distinctive features which American English was later to develop.

Next, what was the general state of Elizabethan English? The population of England in Shakespeare's time has been estimated at 4,460,000. In 1600, probably 200,000 people lived in London, the prestige of which tended to make the regional dialect into a standard for the English-speaking world. (But even London, today, has the strangely non-standard dialect called Cockney, a memorial to the different speechways of seafaring men around a port.)

Naturally any variety of Elizabethan English would sound somewhat different from any twentieth-century counterpart. Certain, though not all, of these differences may provide us with a partial explanation of the current variations in the pronunciation between British and American English. For one thing, many words which are now pronounced with the vowel of *meat* had, at the time of the earliest settlements in America, the quality of present-day English *mate*. In fact, Londoners were accustomed to hear both the *ee* and the *ay* sounds in such words as *meat, teach, sea, tea, lean,* and *beard.* The conservative *ay* pronunciation continued in the language as late as the time of Alexander Pope. On occasion, Shakespeare was capable of rhyming *please* with *knees* and at other times with *grace*. Without this double pronunciation a speech such as that by Dromio in *The Comedy of Errors,* "Marry sir, she's the Kitchin wench, & al *grease* (*grace*)" would have lost its punning effect.

It is also possible that words which today have the vowel of *mate* were pronounced at times with the vowel of *sand*. There is in *All's Well That Ends Well* another punning passage involving a common or highly similar pronunciation of *grace* and *grass:*

CLOWN.   Indeed sir she was the sweete margerom of the sallet or rather the hearbe of grace.

LAFEW.   They are not hearbes you knave, they are nose-hearbes.

CLOWN.   I am no great Nebuchadnezar, sir, I have not much skill in grace.

A secular generation may need to be reminded that Nebuchadnezar, once stricken by the Lord, ate (and "became skilled in") grass.

There was undoubtedly quite as much fluctuation in words which are generally spelled with *oo* (the classes of *food, good,* and *flood*). It is only recently that the pronunciation of many of these words has become standardized. All three of these words constitute one of Shakespeare's rhymes, and a half-century later Dryden rhymed *flood* with *mood* and *good*. Even today certain words of this class (*roof, room, root, hoof, coop, soot,* etc.) are pronounced variously in different parts of the United States.

At the time of which we are writing, the vowel of *cut* had recently developed in London speech and was not yet a feature of all the English dialects. Combinations of *ir, er,* and *ur* in words like *bird, learn,* and *turn* had not long before coalesced into a vowel which was more like the sound to be heard over most of the United States today than that which is characteristic of southern British English. Contemporary pronunciation was far from settled in words like *clerk,* which seems to have been classed part of the time with the sound of *dark* and at other times with the sound of *jerk*. Moreover, this variation affected many more words than it does now. Shakespeare rhymed *convert* with *art*, *serve* with *carve*, and *heard* with *regard*.

In addition, the language at that time had no sound like the stressed vowel of present-day *father* or *calm*. The diphthongs characteristic of such words as *house* and *loud* had, instead of the *ah* first element commonly employed today, a sound somewhat like the final vowel of *Cuba*. The whole diphthong was pronounced in a manner quite similar to that which may be heard at the present time in tidewater Virginia or in the Toronto area of Canada. The diphthong in words like *bite* and *bide* (long *i*) had historically been much like the vowel of present-day *mate*. Thus, seventeenth century *rice* did not rhyme with twentieth-century *ice* but was much closer to our pronunciation of *race*. It was this form (spelled *res* in transcriptions by linguists) that we find in a present-day English-based Creole language, Sranan Tongo of Suriname, where the seventeenth-century maritime pronunciation is in a sense fossilized. The so-called short *o* sound of *cot* and *fog* was always pronounced with the lips somewhat rounded, as in modern English *fall*.

Nor were the stress patterns of Shakespeare's English absolutely identical with those of the modern period. A line such as "The light will show, character'd in my brow," indicates that in such a trisyllabic word as *character'd,* the stress had not yet shifted to the first syllable. A good many two-syllable words which now stress the first, at that time had the accent on the second. Note, "And there I'll rest, as after much *turmoil*." Many derivatives in *-able* had a distinct stress, at least secondary in value, on the suffix. A line such as "What *acceptable* audit canst thou leave?" clearly indicates this stress.

Many words show a double stress pattern: *sincere* with stress at times on the first and at times on the second syllable; *confiscate* on occasion has initial stress, and elsewhere on the second syllable. It is probably fair to say that just as with vowel quality, the language during the Elizabethan period permitted somewhat more latitude than it does today (at least in the "standard" dialect).

It must be kept in mind, moreover, that the pronunciations which have just been discussed reflect only the language practices of the inhabitants of London and its environs, constituting approximately five per cent of the five million who spoke English at that time. The remaining ninety-five per cent spoke regional or provincial dialects—in addition to special varieties if they took to the sea or traveled much. Those who live in the United States may find it hard to conceive of the extent to which regional dialects differ, even today, within an area no larger than one of our moderate-size states. Nor do we find it easy to appreciate the problems of language accommodation and dialect adaptation for a heterogeneous group of emigrants formed of speakers from a number of those widely diverse dialect regions.

At the present time, to select just a single instance, a word such as *about* will be pronounced with the stressed vowel of *bite* in Devon, with the vowel of *boot* along the Scottish border, with the vowel of *father* and a final consonant more like *d* than *t* in London Cockney, and with a pronunciation something like *abaeut* in Norfolk.

To anyone in the United States who has grown up in a tradition of relative linguistic uniformity (with extremes of non-standard dialects limited to social distribution or confined to the Georgia– South Carolina Low Country) over a territory virtually three million square miles in area, such differences in speech present in a country only one-sixtieth as large are startling, to say the least. But in the England of today, regional dialects are confined to a relatively small portion of the population as compared with those of three centuries ago. There can be little question about the wide prevalence of dialect, and the general lack of uniformity of speech, with which the American settlers at the end of the seventeenth century had to cope. That fact alone ensures an interesting and complex history for early American English.

Seventeenth-century English differed from its modern counterpart in other aspects of speech as well. Although the language had in general developed most of the inflections which are used in present-day English—the noun plurals, the object form *them* in the plural pronoun, the past tense and past participle forms of the regular verb—a few interesting earlier features still remained. Among these were the double forms of the pronoun of address: *thou* and *ye* or *you*. Because the distribution of these was governed partly by considerations of social rank and partly on the basis of emotional overtones, their very presence in the language made for a subtlety which today must be achieved through quite different means. It should be noted, however, that nonstandard American dialects often try to produce a second-person plural pronoun: *you all* (*y'awl*), *youse, yez guys*, even Gullah *wuna*.

Note, in the following well-known passage from the first part of *Henry IV*, how the choice of pronouns reflects Hotspur's shift of mood from jesting to sternness through his shift from familiar *thou/thee* to the more impersonal *you*.

> Come, wilt *thou* see me ride?
> And when I am o'horseback, I will swear
> I love *thee* infinitely. But hark *you*, Kate;
> I must not have *you* henceforth question me.

Actually, at one point slightly later than Shakespeare's time, this matter of the second personal pronoun became a politico-religious issue. The Quakers, committed to a belief in the innate equality of all men, interpreted the duality of the pronoun of address as a negation of that equality and argued, quite intemperately at times, for a return to an older state of the language where the two forms were differentiated solely on the basis of number. It is worth noting that the English language did eventually go along with Quaker leader George Fox's democratic prescriptions by giving up the pronoun differentiation based upon social status (*you* to persons of high rank, *thou* to those lower on the scale), but in so doing, ironically selected the form which Fox considered inappropriate for the task (the old plural, *you*, which came to be used in the singular).

This double supply of pronouns also carried with it an accompanying difference in verb structure, for *thou* as subject regularly demanded a verb ending in *-est*. *Ye* or *you* as subject was accompanied merely by the simple or root form of the verb. Thus we would have at this time *thou teachest* but *you teach, thou knowest* but *you* or *ye know*. After the *thou* forms fell into disfavor, except in certain discourse types like prayer, so too did the verb inflections in *-est,* leaving the second person singular of the verb identical with the first person and with all forms of the plural.

In addition, Elizabethan English represents a period of change from an earlier *-eth* inflection for the third person singular of the verb to the *-s* forms characteristic of the language today. There is an interesting difference here between the practice of Shakespeare and that of the contemporary King James Version of the Bible. The latter regularly uses *-eth:* "He maketh me to lie down in green pastures." In his ordinary dramatic prose, Shakespeare employs *-s* regularly for all verbs except *have* and *do,* which retain the archaic *hath* and *doth* (the latter only occasionally) presumably because these were learned as individual forms early in life by the average speaker instead of as part of an over-all pattern. There is some evidence, however, from works like Richard Hodges's *A Special Help to Orthographie,* that by the seventeenth century spellings like *roweth* and *rose, wrights* and *righteth,* (Mr.) *Knox* and *knocketh* represented an orthographic tradition only and not a universal pronunciation of standard British English. There is no real evidence that the *-eth* ending for the third person singular verb played any significant part in the history of American English.

One way to acquire a feeling for many of the differences between the standard language of today and that of the Elizabethan Age is to observe with care a selection of one of the earliest examples of what might be called American English. The following selection, from William Bradford's *History of Plimmoth Plantation,* will serve the purpose:

In these hard and difficulte beginnings they found some discontents and murmurings arise amongst some, and mutinous speeches and carriages in other; but they were soone quelled and overcome by the wisdome, patience, and just and equall carrage of things by the Gov[erno]r and better part, which clave faithfully togeather in the maine. But that which was most sadd and lamentable was, that in 2 or 3 moneths time halfe of their company dyed, espetialy in Jan: and February, being the depth of winter, and wanting houses and other comforts; being infected with the scurvie and other diseases, which this long voiage and their inacomodate condition had brought upon them; so as ther dyed some times 2 or 3 of a day, in the aforesaid time; that of 100 and odd persons, scarce 50 remained. And of these in the time of most distres, ther was but 6 or 7 sound persons, who, to their great comendations be it spoken, spared no pains, night nor day, but with abundance of toil and hazard of their owne health, fetched them woode, made them fires, drest them meat, made their beads, washed their lothsome cloaths, cloathed and uncloathed them; in a word, did all the homly and necessarye offices for them which dainty and quesie stomacks cannot endure to hear named; and all this willingly and cherfully, without any grudging in the least, shewing herin their true love unto their freinds and bretheren. A rare example and worthy to be remembered. Tow of these 7 were Mr. William Brewster, ther reverend Elder, and Myles Standish, ther Captein and Military comander, unto whom my selfe, and many others, were much beholden in our low and sicke condition. And yet the Lord so upheld these persons, as in this generall calamity they were not at all infected either with sickness, or lamnes. And what I have said of these, I may say of many others who dyed in this generall visitation, and others yet living, that whilst they had health, yea, or any strength continuing, they were not wanting to any that had need of them. And I doute not but their recompence is with the Lord.

But I may not hear pass by an other remarkable passage not to be forgotten. As this calamitie fell among the passengers that were to be left here to plant, and were hasted a shore and made to drinke water, that the sea-men might have the more bear, and one in his sickness desiring but a small cann of beere, it was answered, that if he were their owne father he should have none; the disease begane to fall amongst them also, so as allmost halfe of their company dyed before they went away, and many of their officers and lustyest men, as the boatson, gunner, 3 quarter-maisters, the cooke, and others. At which the m[aste]r was something strucken and sent to the sick a shore and tould the Gov[erno]r he should send for beer for them that had need of it, though he drunke water homward bound.

Most noticeable, perhaps, in the passage just quoted are a number of words no longer current in the language. Among them are *inacomodate* and *hasted*. *Yea, unto,* and *beholden* are rarely employed except in certain set phrases and at times in religious connections. Other words have come to be used in contexts quite unlike those in which they appear in this passage. For instance, *carriages* no longer signifies behavior in the abstract sense; *clothed,* here meaning the specific act of dressing, has become more general in its use. *Offices* is used here in the sense of services; *lustiest* to mean healthiest. Though by no means inclusive, these examples suggest the changes which have taken place in the English vocabulary during the last three centuries, both with respect to the words it comprises and the meanings of these words.

Likewise, certain changes in the forms of words have taken place. Almost at the beginning of the passage, *other* was used as a plural pronoun, although the modern form *others* appears later on. *Scarce,* in an adverbial use, indicates that the fetish of the *-ly* ending was somewhat less strong at that time than it is at present. As might be expected, the most pronounced differences are in the verb forms, where *clave* and *drunke* appear as past tenses and *strucken* as a past participle.

Differences in syntax are even more numerous. The plural form of the abstractions *discontents* and *murmurings* would be unlikely to appear in present-day usage, as would *commendations.* Closely connected with this same problem of number is the lack of agreement between subject and verb in, "There was but 6 or 7 sound persons." The word *as* in constructions like "so as ther dyed," and "as in this generall calamity," would today be replaced by *that.* At the same time, certain pronominal uses of *that* in this selection would unquestionably call for *who* in the language of today.

Even more striking than any of these features is the sentence structure. In general the sentences, even though they are part of a rather carefully prepared text, differ markedly from the surface structure of edited prose in the twentieth century. Bradford felt no

compulsion to avoid phrases and clauses which modern handbooks would call "dangling." The first sentence in the selection
contains fifty-three words, the second eighty-three, and the third
attains a total of one hundred and six. These are all long according to modern standards, even if there is no absolutely reliable
method of specifying the maximum length of a sentence. Ironically, the third sentence is followed by an eight-word fragment
that does not fit the modern pattern of the conventional sentence
at all. In the second sentence the parallelism of the phrases introduced by *being* and *wanting* is faulty and would not gladden
the heart of a twentieth-century composition teacher. The majority of the sentences are without coherence and direction in the
present sense of these terms.

The proper conclusion, however, is not that Bradford was a bad
writer—in fact he was not—but that there were differences between seventeenth-century prose and our own. Some of these differences are purely a matter of historical development. The roots
of our modern forms and practices were already in the language.
It is even more important to recognize this as a period prior to a
certain codification, or settlement, one might almost say a jelling,
of English written prose. A man's spelling was still his own concern, as is clearly evident, and so too, to some extent, were his
sentences. If this codification or jelling took place after the two
main speech areas, England and America, were already separated,
it is more than possible that the settling processes might not work
out in the same way in both places.

But the prose writings of relatively educated persons are far
from the whole story about any language. Bradford himself reports something about the speech of an Indian named Squanto
and his friend, whose special language variety was "American English," at least in the special sense that it was certainly non-British.
Bradford quoted nothing from the Indians, but later writers gave
us examples of American Indian Pidgin English like "What much
hoggery!" (a response to shelling by British naval boats) which
John Underhill, in *Newes from America* of 1638, translated as

"How angry!" Although the phonology of *hoggery* from *angry* is strange, modern scholars have accepted Underhill's statement. This means that, in the Pidgin English, *angry*—an adjective in English—is modified by *much,* which is a noun modifier in the source language. This quotation, in Pidgin, is one of the first examples of the functional shift which became such an important factor in the formation of the American vocabulary. A slightly later attestation in Pidgin English has an Indian saying, "Um, umh poo[r] Ingismon, mee save you life, no take you to Captain Mosee [Mosely]." There are very many such quotations in the colonial records.

Since the earliest American settlers employed "Elizabethan English"—in whatever special varieties may have existed at that time—it is the highly variable and complex character of that medium that provides us with an explanation of the beginning of the divergence in the two major streams of our language. It remains to be seen how, and through what means, this divergence developed throughout the course of the intervening centuries.

With all this complexity, it becomes a serious problem to determine whether there is an overall pattern, or patterns, in American English. Perhaps the most important clue will prove to be the state of the English language at the time when the English-speaking colonies were first established in the New World.

3
Languages and Cultures in Contact

Considered from the point of view of vocabulary, there are few, if any, "pure" languages. Historically, English has been notorious as a word borrower, but it is equally true that every Western European language has supplemented its lexicon by adoptions from other languages. In this respect then, English was like the other immigrant languages brought to the New World, and in a broader sense, like every other language that has ever existed. Loan words occur even in the languages of aboriginal peoples. Even Indo-European, the hypothetical parent of most of the languages found in Europe today and many of those in western Asia, appears to have borrowed words some 4000 years ago from Finno-Ugric, and to have furnished others in return. In the same manner, American Indian languages soon picked up European words like *kabay* (a variant of Romance language *caballo, cheval,* etc.) for "horse," and the international European vocabulary soon had words like *canoe, tobacco,* and *hammock* from the Indians.

One great impetus toward word borrowing arises from the necessity of talking about new things, qualities, operations, concepts, and ideas. Inevitably the movement of a people to a markedly different environment not only creates a problem of communication but makes it an urgent requirement. Almost as soon as he struck land, Columbus "seized by force several Indians on the first island in order that they might learn from us, and in like manner tell us about those things in these lands of which they themselves had knowledge; and the plan succeeded, for in a short time we understood them and they us, sometimes by gesture and signs, sometimes by words; and it was a great advantage to us." None of the early reporters tell us, however, the answer to the most interesting question for language historians: What were those words (and gestures), and how did the interlocutors put them together?

We do know that the migration of the English to North America, the first stage in what was to culminate in a dramatic sweep across the continent, posed quite the same problems and created the same vocabulary need that Columbus and his men experienced. We know too that, even earlier than Columbus, Mediterranean sailors had faced the same problems and had worked out a solution by creating a common language, the Lingua Franca. The members of the Smith and Bradford companies who put themselves ashore in Virginia and Massachusetts, respectively, encountered not only plants, fish, and animals new to them but found themselves among tribes of indigenous peoples who spoke strange languages, wore strange clothing, prepared strange foods (like *hominy*), and maintained tribal customs quite different from anything the English had previously encountered. Even the landscape was different from the neatly tailored English countryside. Names had to be provided for all these unfamiliar aspects of their new life.

The same situation was constantly repeated, for all European settlers, as colonization proceeded westward (or northward). The flora and fauna of the prairie states, the deep South, the Rocky Mountain area, the Southwest, and the Pacific coast presented a different appearance and therefore required new names. The Indian tribes, their languages, and their customs also presented naming problems, as did other features of colonial and frontier life.

Among the relatively early expeditions to the West, the Lewis and Clark expedition, ostensibly political and economic in purpose, also had a scientific aim. President Jefferson, a man of wide curiosity, was eager to learn as much as possible about the newly acquired Louisiana Purchase, and therefore assigned the leaders the task of ascertaining the geography of the country, the nature and customs of the Indian nations, the plants, animals, mineral resources, and the climate. It was quite natural then to find in the notebooks of the expedition party such statements as "These natives have a large quantity of this root bread which they call *commass* [camass]," and that subsequent references to the plant would employ the same word.

I Indian Influence

The Lewis and Clark expedition came after 1803, but politically unsanctioned trappers ("mountain men"), hunters, and land grabbers had preceded them by decades. In their rudely informal way, these earlier groups had found out a lot about the Indians, including the many languages spoken by the diverse tribes. The mountain man did not have the same missionary purpose in learning the language as did Roger Williams, but the influence of what he learned may have been, in the long run, more significant.

Modern scholars think in terms of hundreds of languages spoken by the Indians who lived in what is now the Continental United States, although the number has been revised downward somewhat in the last decade. These languages can be put into genetic groupings much as Swedish, Norwegian, Dutch, and English are put into the Germanic branch of the Indo-European family by more traditional reconstructionists. For our purposes, it is enough to know that the English-speaking settlers came into contact with a large number of different languages, although the actual number of speakers per language may have been relatively small. In pre-Columbian times, some of the Indian groups had experienced problems with this diversity of native languages and had worked out special contact language (pidgin) solutions: Pidginized Algonquian and Huron; Delaware Jargon; Pidgin Ojibway; Mobilian Jargon or "Yama" (from the word for "yes") of the Gulf States; Chinook Jargon of the Northwest; and the sign language of the Plains Indians.

The genetic classification of American Indian languages has changed greatly within the last few years. It is hardly necessary to go into the technical details of the classifications here. Older works, including the *Dictionary of Americanisms* and other reference books, stressed groups like the Algonquian (including Narragansett, Massachusetts, and Penobscot, spoken in New England; Virginian and Powhatan in the South; and Ojibwa and Pottawatomi in the central West), the Iroquoian (distributed chiefly throughout New York, Pennsylvania, and Ohio), Siouan (chiefly in the plains area west of the Mississippi), Uto-Aztecan (penetrating deep into Mexico), and Penutian (the languages of the great Northwest). Some of these classifications would not please the most advanced scholars, but they are familiar and sufficiently useful for our purposes. The important thing to remember is that these languages furnished most of the American Indian words taken into English.

In order to understand certain aspects of the borrowing process we must know something about the nature of these languages. Many of them contain sounds which do not occur in English: series of nasalized vowels and various kinds of pharyngealized and glottalized consonants. Speakers of English would tend to approximate such sounds rather than to reproduce them. There were also frequent combinations of consonants absent from English, such as the initial clusters in the following Ojibway words: *mtik, pshikye, kchimkwa*. The English speakers encountering such combinations as these would in all probability eliminate one of the consonants, or else insert vowels between them. Early English usage of the Indian loan words varied considerably and was established only with time.

Moreover, most of the Indian languages are of the so-called incorporating or "agglutinative" type insofar as word-formation is concerned. They tend to put together in a single word a great many elements which in English are separate lexical units. Inflectionally, they use not only suffixes and prefixes but infixes as well. William Penn's description, technically inexact to be sure, reflects the impression that these languages made on many of the Englishmen who found it necessary to bridge the communication gap:

> Their *Language* is lofty, yet narrow, but like the *Hebrew;* in Signification full; like *Short-hand* in writing; *one* word serveth in the place of *three,* and the rest are supplied by the understanding of the Hearer: Imperfect in their *Tenses,* wanting in their *Moods, Participles, Adverbs, Conjunctions, Interjections:* I have made it my business to understand it, that I might not want an interpreter on any occasion: And I must say, that I know not a Language spoken in *Europe,* that hath words of more sweetness or greatness, in *Accent* and *Emphasis,* than theirs.

Many another English-speaking observer compared the Indian languages to Hebrew, reflecting the prevalent theory that the American aboriginals were somehow the descendants of the lost tribes of Israel. The appeals to Latin grammatical categories and to euphony were generally characteristic of amateur linguistic description of the period. But even through such description it is possible to see the comprehensive difficulties encountered by the English and it is not surprising, therefore, that Indian words would be changed considerably, both in form and meaning, as a result of the borrowing process.

The following list contains the principal loan words in present-day American English from the various Indian languages of the North American continent, classified according to the aspects of life and fields of activity they represent.

This list of American Indian borrowings comprises about fifty words, but it should be noted that compounds and larger expressions ("idioms") would greatly increase the list. It should also be noted that the items are restricted to those which might be consid-

Trees, Plants, Fruits

catalpa
catawba
hickory
pecan
persimmon
poke (-berry, -weed)
scuppernong
sequoia
squash
tamarack

Animals

cayuse
chipmunk
moose
muskrat
opossum
raccoon
skunk
terrapin
woodchuck

Fish

menhaden
muskellunge
porgy *
quahog

Foods

hominy
hooch
pemmican
pone
succotash
supawn

Amerindian Culture

manitou
potlatch
powwow
sachem
skookum
totem

papoose
squaw

mackinaw
moccasin
tomahawk
wampum

hogan
igloo
kayak
tepee
wigwam

Political Terms

caucus †
mugwump
Tammany

Miscellaneous

chautauqua
chinook
podunk

* This probably represents a mixed derivation or confusion of Spanish *pargo* and a form *paugie* of Narragansett origin.
† The Amerindian origin of this word has recently been called into question. Since no convincing case has been put forward for any other specific derivation, it is included here.

ered part of the vocabulary of a large number of speakers of American English, and that Southwestern borrowings from Indian languages, like *coyote* and *tomato,* are not included here.

Certain difficulties present themselves in selectively including only those words known to most Americans. Often plant and animal names are current only within the regions where the objects themselves are to be found. Thus *scuppernong, cayuse,* and *menhaden* are likely to be better known in the coastal South, the West, and New England respectively than in other parts of the country. In the Northwest, words from Chinook Jargon like *skookum, siwash* (ultimately from French *sauvage*), *chinook* itself (a wind) are generally known, and the language of loggers in the woods of Washington and Oregon contains many words "from the Indian." On the other hand, a few words, like *squaw* and *papoose,* were carried out to the Far West and may even be internationally known. Certain other words, such as *quahog* and *supawn,* are unusually localized in their distribution and may have alternate terms even within the relatively restricted area where they are current. *Quahog,* for example, to some speakers may be *round clam, hardshell clam,* or *hen clam. Hasty pudding, Indian pudding, Indian meal pudding,* and *mush* are all lexical variants of *supawn* in the Hudson Valley.

Many of the Indian borrowings are now disappearing from the language. It was not so long ago that *kinnikinnick* and *poggamoggan* were as familiar at least as the term *pemmican.* The Unami word *nitape* "my friend, fellow tribesman" was diffused throughout American Indian Pidgin English and Delaware Jargon and was widely known in the late eighteenth and early nineteenth centuries to monolingual English speakers on the East Coast. It showed up also in Powhatan, an Algonquian language of Virginia. How rapidly some Indian words are dropping from the language is dramatically illustrated by a listing, made in 1902, of borrowings from the Algonquian languages alone. The list contains 132 words. By 1958, not more than thirty-seven of them were in use. In the intervening twenty-odd years, others on the list have become even less familiar.

The domains, or spheres of life, represented by the borrowings show that the largest number of loan words are connected with Indian institutions and civilization. Here it was obviously easier to borrow the Indian term than to create a new one out of English elements. For the most part the remaining words are the names of plants, animals, and foods which the colonists found in the New World and which were new to them.

Of the fifty-two words included in the list, approximately three-quarters have been derived from one or another of the Algonquian languages. Among the other families represented are Muskhoghian, Iroquois, Sioux, Penutian, and Eskimo, but no one of them is represented by more than three words. This overwhelming influence of the Algonquian may be explained in part by the fact that these languages were the first to be encountered by the white men as they settled on the Atlantic coast, and in part by their early adoption into Pidgin English, which provided for their spread across the nation. Once the Algonquian terms had been applied to the unfamiliar flora, fauna, and Indian institutions, they tended to remain in the language, even though words from other language families were encountered later on. Although cowboys and trappers often piously believed that they were "speaking the Indians' language," to the Indians themselves these were "white men's words."

Wigwam, an Algonquian term for an Indian house or tent, appears in English as early as 1628, not long after the beginning of the New England colonization. A somewhat different type of lodge, usually conical in shape and more likely to be constructed of skins, was the *tepee* of the plains Indians. The first citation for this is 1835, at a time when explorers and settlers were pushing across the Mississippi. *Hogan,* the Navaho word for a dwelling built of earth and supported by upright or slanting timbers, does not put in an appearance until 1871. Here the various objects differed from each other to a degree, but *wigwam,* the earliest of the borrowings, was frequently used as a synonym for the others. In fact, *wigwam words* was an early term for American English expressions that reflected real or fancied Indian influence.

It is also noteworthy that word borrowing from the Indians began very early. *Moose, raccoon, opossum, terrapin,* and *persimmon* are all recorded prior to the landing of the Pilgrims. *Powwow, sachem, wigwam,* and *musquash* (the earlier form of *muskrat*) were in the language before the founding of the Massachusetts Bay Colony. On the whole, just about one-half of all the American Indian loan words now current in the language became a part of it during the seventeenth century; the other half may be divided about equally between eighteenth-century and nineteenth-century adoptions. There were many more later borrowings of course—sixty-seven have been found in the journals of the members of the Lewis and Clark expedition alone—but many of these words, such as *wapatoo, carkajou,* and *salal,* were of short duration in the English language.

Some of the structural peculiarities of the American Indian languages and the unusual sounds and combinations of sounds they employed have already been mentioned. Since most languages tend to remake or re-form borrowed words in their own general structure, it was natural that these words should have been changed considerably in language contact, usually in the direction of simplification or shortening, in order to be more easily used by speakers of another language or languages. According to Roger Williams, the Narrangansett word which gave rise to present English *menhaden* was *munnawhatteag. Wampum* is an abbreviated form of *wampampeag. Squash* appears to have been shortened from a Narragansett *askutasquash.* Raccoon shows up as *raughroughcums* in Captain John Smith's *True Relation,* and was apparently derived from a Virginian *arahkunem.* Thus it is apparent that either or both ends of a word might be lopped off in the course of the borrowing process. Just how much the actual sounds themselves were altered, we will probably never know, since the earliest records of the American Indian languages antedate the development of modern phonetic science.

One other type of change may occur in the form of a loan word, the result of a psychological rather than a phonetic process. This is particularly well illustrated by the term *woodchuck,* which seems to have had its origin in a Cree or Ojibwa word appearing variously as *wuchak, otchak, odjig,* meaning "fisher" or "weasel." It was, at any rate, an animal which bore some association with the woods, and presumably to give a semblance of reason to this strange combination of sounds, the English-speaking colonists converted the first syllable into *wood.* This type of modification, arising from a popular or unlearned effort to resolve a strange or unusual word into understandable elements, is called folk or popular etymology.

Other possible instances of folk etymology among the Amerindian loan words is *muskrat,* a rodent with a musky odor, called *muskwessu* or *muscassus,* in the Algonquian languages. *Musquash,* the direct reflex of the etymological form, is still regularly employed in England, but the American *muskrat* certainly suggests a reworking of the word in an effort to lend some sense to the component parts. *Chipmunk,* from an Ojibwa *achitam,* may represent the same process. Among Indian words no longer current, Narragansett *wattap,* "string roots of spruce used for sewing canoes," often appeared as *watape* or *way-tape.*

In words borrowed from such familiar languages as Latin, French, and Italian, there is often a reasonably close correspondence between the meaning of the word in English and in the language from which it was borrowed. Thus *nocturnal, consommé,* and *cupola* have the same meaning in English that they have or had in the languages from which they were taken. It should be remembered, however, that the relationship between English and those languages was often one of mutual bilingualism, and that all the languages concerned had a long tradition of literacy. Because the Indian languages were usually encountered in a polyglot, rough-and-tumble context of oral exchange, the actual conversation frequently took place in a simplified (pidginized) form of the source language. Thus *squash* is a clipped form of the original Narrangansett word *askutasquash,* meaning literally "vegetables eaten green." *Succotash* is taken from *misikquatash*, also Narragansett, which signified "the grains are whole." Virginian *pawcohiccora*, the original form of *hickory*, was a term applied to a hickory or walnut kernel mush, and the word which gave rise to present-day *moose* meant "he strips or eats off."

Loan words not only alter their meaning in the course of the language contact process, but they are equally liable to change after they have become a naturalized part of the English language. *Powwow*, one of the very early American Indian adoptions, originally bore its etymological meaning of priest or medicine man. Less than fifty years from the time of its first appearance in English it was applied to a ceremony in which magic was practiced and feasting and dancing indulged in. About a century later it changed its meaning to that of a council held by Indians or a conference with them, presumably because feasting and dancing were an integral part of such conclaves. After another half-century (1812), the word was so generalized that it was variously applied to political or scientific conferences, friendly consultations, or a palaver of any kind. This final development was actually anticipated by the verb *to powwow*, which was formed from the noun very soon after its adoption into the language.

Equally interesting is the semantic development of *mugwump*. It came from *mugquomp*, a Natick word meaning "great chief," and John Eliot in his *Massachusetts Bible* used it to translate *duke* in Genesis xxvi.15. By 1832 the word had acquired an aura of playfulness and jocularity, as illustrated by a citation mentioning the "most Worshipful Mugwumps of the Cabletow." In 1884 it was specifically applied by the regular Republicans to those bolters from the party who refused to accept James Blaine as the presidential candidate, throwing their support to Grover Cleveland, the Democratic nominee. The element of ridicule and irony intended here may well have gone awry, for Cleveland and not Blaine won the election. At any rate it has since been used, often in a thoroughly complimentary fashion, to indicate an independent in politics, though the recent folk-etymology analysis of the term, as one who has his "mug" on one side of the fence and his "wump" on the other, has again given it a jocular and somewhat unfavorable connotation.

Sachem illustrates a similar development. It originally meant the head of a particular confederation, but it soon changed to the generalized meaning of any great man. This in turn has been specialized to apply to the head of the old Tammany Hall political organization of New York, which itself was named for an Indian chief.

It is well known that large numbers of place names in the United States—names of cities, states, counties, islands, rivers and lakes—are taken from the Indian languages. *Chicago,* for example, came from an Algonquian word meaning "garlic field." Some of these place names later developed an interesting type of meaning change. *Mackinaw,* the name of the island at the junction of Lakes Huron and Michigan, according to one explanation at least, was a shortening of *Michilimackinac,* meaning "great turtle." The reason for this application is clear enough to anyone who has suddenly come upon the pine-wooded hills of the island projecting from the water. Under both the British and the American administrations Mackinaw was the seat of an Indian agency. Here the United States government distributed, among other things, blankets to the Indians, who had a decided preference for plaids, checks, and bright colors. Thus, highly colored blankets intended for Indian distribution came to be known as *Mackinaw blankets.* After the northern part of Michigan became a lumbering center, such blankets frequently furnished the material for short jackets worn by the lumbermen. These were first called *Mackinaw coats* and finally just *mackinaws.*

Tribal names underwent the same type of development. *Catawba,* meaning "separated," was applied in turn to a Siouan tribe living in Carolina, then to a grape grown in that particular area, next to the wine made from the grape, and finally to the red color characteristic of the wine. *Chinook,* also originally a tribal label, has become the name of a language (and, in *Chinook Jargon,* of a contact variety), two different kinds of winds, and a variety of salmon. Other words present equally fascinating stories of change in meaning, but these should be sufficient to make the point that once a foreign word is adopted into a language, it is liable to the application of all the forces making for semantic development and alteration in that language.

All the Amerindian loan words are nouns, indicating in a sense the most superficial type of borrowing, and reflecting a casual rather than intimate mingling of the two cultures. In Pidgin English and in other contact languages, however, words change their grammatical functions quite readily. (The same process occurs, although not so extensively, in standard English.) Many of the Indian borrowings have subsequently been used as verbs: *caucus, powwow, tomahawk, hickory, skunk* (in a slang sense), *wigwam, potlatch,* and *mugwump.* These eight borrowings are still widely used although the last three are rarely used as verbs. In general, verbal use is attested not long after the original noun adoption: within half a century in the case of most of these, and sometimes in considerably less time.

Even more significant for evaluating the total influence of the Indian languages is the fact that most of the borrowed nouns entered readily into compound-word combinations. Webster's *New International Dictionary,* 1971, listed fifteen compounds for *hickory,* fourteen for *squaw,* and twelve for *skunk. Poke* exists only in such combinations as *pokeweed* and *pokeberry.* Sometimes the compounds are triple in nature, as in *hickory bark beetle* and *hickory horned devil.*

Certain of these borrowings, although they do not combine extensively with other full words, do show a strong tendency toward the attachment of derivative prefixes and suffixes, particularly the latter. Thus *caucus* gave rise to *caucusable, caucusdom, caucuser,* and *caucusified,* to say nothing of *caucusing* as a verbal noun. From *mugwump* came *mugwumpery, mugwumpian, mugwumpey,* and *mugwumpism;* from *skunk* came *skunkery, skunkish,* and *skunky. Tammany* gave us *Tammanyism, Tammanyite, Tammanyize,* and *Tammanize.* Few of these are part of the everyday

American vocabulary in 1980, but they do illustrate the early impact of a group of borrowed words on the language. By the time all functional changes, compounds, and derivatives are taken into account, something less than fifty loan words have added many times that number of lexical units to the language. According to one estimate, present-day English contains some 1700 words from the Indian languages. It is doubtful if any figure can be authoritatively set, but the important point to recognize is that the increase over the actual number of words directly borrowed comes as a result of the processes just discussed.

In addition to the impact upon English produced by the direct borrowings from the Amerindian languages, there were also results of a somewhat less direct nature. Most obvious of these are the many compounds with the word *Indian* as a first element: *Indian file, Indian sign, Indian physic,* even *Indian whiskey.* The last of these developed in association with a very un-Indian term, *bootlegger.* The trading of whiskey to the Indians (selling "Indian whiskey") was prohibited, and smugglers developed small, flat bottles that could be carried in the leg of a boot. The *Dictionary of Americanisms* lists eighty *Indian-* compounds, with *Indian field* (1634) and *Indian meal* (1635) the earliest. Later examples include *Indian claim, Indian summer, Indian gift* and *giver, Indian creeper,* and *Indian cucumber.*

Another Amerindian influence may be seen in certain word or phrase combinations which would appear to be the translation into native elements of real or imagined Indian compounds. *Firewater,* for example, is apparently a literal translation of an Algonquian *scoutiouabou* (*ishkotéwabó* in Father Frederic Baraga's Ojibway grammar). It is difficult to say whether the many compounds with *war* (*-chief, -club, -party, -path,* etc.) are all translations of actual Indian terms. Combinations such as *maiaoséwinini,* "war chief," did exist in some of the languages, but no evidence exists to indicate whether the English formation is a literal translation or a vocabulary innovation within American Indian Pidgin English. Ojibwa *wâbinêsiwin* did mean "paleness of the face"; it may well have been the source of the widely attested *paleface*. Phrases like *great* or *big water* ("ocean"), *Great Spirit* ("God"), and *Great White Father* are all well attested in early Pidgin documents, and characteristic of the entire language contact picture where the Indians are concerned. Mobilian Jargon of the Gulf States has an element *cheto* "big" which acts in much the same way: *takkon* "peach" becomes *takkon cheto* "apple"; *ekhana* "watch" becomes *ekhana cheto* "clock"; *tamaha* "town" becomes *tamaha cheto* "city," etc.

The phrases *bury the hatchet* and *dig* (or *take*) *up the hatchet* are also well attested in early Pidgin documents. All of these have been used in movies and in pulp novels, and the academic world has shown a certain embarrassment—as if genuine usages could be contaminated by such employment. But early travelers, missionaries, and other observers attest even the use of *"How!"* as a ritual utterance if not exactly as a greeting.

II French Influence

Besides the various Indian influences, American English reflects the other non-English cultures which the colonists and frontiersmen met in their conquest of the continent. In the westward expansion of their territory, the English-speaking colonists soon came into contact with the French. Explorers, trappers, traders, and missionaries had streamed into the valleys of the St. Lawrence and the Mississippi, following hard upon the trail of Champlain and La-Salle. By 1700 the French held virtually all the strategic posts along these great rivers and a number of vital points on the shores of the Great Lakes as well.

This was the world of the *voyageurs*, the *coureurs de(s) bois*, and the *habitants*—a riotous and colorful frontier, invaded twice a year by rough, simple, and hairy woods runners, either en route to trap the furs which were so vital to the economy of the French (and interacting with the American mountain men in the process), or returning triumphantly with their booty.

In striking contrast New Orleans, the center of French influence in this country, was for a long time the most European of American cities. It boasted a prosperous theater which catered to wealthy aristocrats from all over the South. It was this city which in 1808 introduced grand opera to America. A distinct though somewhat derivative architecture and an excellent cuisine contributed to its metropolitan atmosphere.

But New Orleans was also a port city, with sailors of all nationalities who corresponded to the frontier rowdies. In New Orleans itself and the surrounding country, a Creole French (sometimes called "Gumbo") alternated with standard French. At least one well-known French borrowing, *lagniappe,* came over the seas (in this case from the Andean Indian language, Quechua) and entered English directly from the "Creole Negroes." The affinities of port life were more nearly with Haiti, Martinique, and Guadeloupe than with the Ile de France.

Thus in their sweep toward the Mississippi, the English encountered a very casual colonial French culture and a fully developed urban one, mediated by a hybrid fitted to Africans and Indians. Standard French had more prestige value than any other language with which the Anglo-Saxons were to come into contact, but the contact variety was probably more useful for many situations of trade and informal interaction.

The words in present-day American English which may be traced to the French in America, classified according to domains, are as follows:

Plants and Animals	Foods
caribou	brioche
crappie	chowder
gopher	jambalaya *
pumpkin	(pie) a la mode

---

* The suggestion of an African origin for this word has been made, and there are a number of Africanisms (like *gris gris*) in Louisiana French. *Jambalaya* is recorded in Modern Provençal—which may be an indication of the power to disperse words of the maritime contact varieties of the colonial period.

praline
sazarac

Toponymics

bayou
butte
chute
coulee
crevasse
flume
levee
prairie
rapids
sault

Furniture and Building

armoire (pronounced like *armor*)
bureau
depot
shanty

Exploration and Travel

bateau
cache

carry-all
pirogue
portage
toboggan
voyageur

Coinage

cent
dime
mill

Miscellaneous

apache
(Indian) brave
Cajun
calumet
Canuck
chambray
charivari
lacrosse
lagniappe
parlay
picayune
rotisserie
sashay

The French loan words are somewhat fewer than those from the American Indian languages, but many of the same problems present themselves in the compilation of what might be considered an authentic list. Such words as *pirogue, coulee, armoire,* and *lagniappe* are distinctly regional in their occurrence. In the same regions, words like *bidet* are familiar to at least some groups in the population—but hardly part of the vocabulary of the general populace. To attempt to deal with such words as Americanisms would involve us in the problem of reborrowing, since English borrowed extensively from Norman French in the period beginning just after 1066. Like the American Indian loan words, many

French borrowings have long since ceased to be an active part of the language. In 1902 Sylva Clapin listed as many as 102 French loan words in his *New Dictionary of Americanisms*. Although some were not French to begin with, others, such as *bogue* (ultimately from Choctaw, the same source as *bayou*), *bagasse*, and *cordelle*, are no longer current. Such forms as *movey star* (*mauvaises terres*), *coteau*, and *bob ruly* (*bois brulé*) would be recognized only along the Canadian border or in Cajun territory.

The French borrowings tend generally to fall into two groups. First, there are a number of words pertaining to exploration and travel, or descriptive of features of the landscape. For the most part these terms result from the contact between English and French in the central states, as did, undoubtedly, such miscellaneous items as *charivari* (regularly pronounced "shivaree" in the United States), *calumet*, and *lacrosse*. On the other hand, food terms like *jambalaya*, *praline*, and *sazarac* suggest the superb chefs, confectioners, and bartenders of the New Orleans area. (A food term like *boudin*, although known in Louisiana and in Canada, is almost completely restricted to areas of direct French influence.) The three coinage terms, *cent*, *dime*, and *mill*, were borrowings from continental rather than colonial French, the first citations appearing in the 1780's, when our monetary system was established largely through the instrumentality of Robert Morris.

Although French was the immediate source of all the words listed here, some of them had originated in other languages. As suggested above, *bayou* was a Choctaw word meaning river or creek. It developed a variety of applications in different parts of the country, depending generally upon the topography and climate. In Texas and the West the word means a deep inlet which affords a channel for the water in times of flood but remains dry or nearly so at other seasons. Along the Mississippi it may be used for an abandoned river course.

Caribou was likewise Indian in origin; it came from Micmac *khalibu*, "pawer or scratcher"; *toboggan* was borrowed by the French from the same language. *Lagniappe*, already said to have come from Quechua, is paralleled by *la ñapa* in Puerto Rican and other Caribbean Spanish and has cognates in Caribbean English dialects. Unfortunately, the practice of giving a little something extra with a purchase is obsolescent, and the word is following the economic practice. In Northwestern Louisiana today, it is seen more frequently as the title of an odds-and-ends section of a folklore newsletter than in all the commercial establishments of the area together. *Parlay,* a term used in connection with gambling and horse racing, is an adaptation by the French of the Italian *paroli.* There were large numbers of Italians among the polyglot settlers of Louisiana, especially in New Orleans.

Unlike the Amerindian loan words, at least half of which came into the language during the seventeenth century, the borrowings from the French appear chiefly during the eighteenth and nineteenth centuries. It is true that *sault* is recorded as early as 1600 in one of Hakluyt's *Voyages,* but the next use of it does not appear until 1809. The earliest citation for *caribou* is 1672; that for *portage* is 1698, in an English translation of the words of Father Louis Hennepin; and *pumpkin, punkin* in informal American speech, is first attested in 1647 from Nathaniel Ward's *The Simple Cobbler of Aggawam.* Except for these, the French loans are divided fairly evenly between the two succeeding centuries. In this connection we must also remember that in the nineteenth century the English language, in general, borrowed more words from continental French than at any time since the period of Norman French influence. These general English borrowings, however, were terms dealing with art, literature, dress, textiles, furniture, and cooking in the main; they have a quite different flavor from the peculiarly American loan words.

In the course of the borrowing process, the French words were by no means as violently distorted in form and pronunciation as were the American Indian terms. Even though the spelling may have been considerably altered at times, as in the case of *gopher* from *gaufre* "honeycomb"—apparently in reference to the digging pattern of those animals—a radical change in pronunciation is not

implied. The most pronounced tendency is to stress the first syllable, or at any rate to shift it forward, as evidenced in *coulee,*
bureau, depot, picayune, and many others in the list, but this has
always been characteristic of the English treatment of French loan
words. English does not have a sound like French *u;* consequently,
the stressed vowels of *butte, flume,* and *bureau* were dealt with according to English phonetic patterns.

Nor is there nearly as much deviation from the etymological
meanings of the French borrowings as was true of the American
Indian loan words. *Praline,* for which the earliest recorded citations are English rather than American but which has since been
used chiefly in the United States, takes its name from the French
marshal whose cook invented the confection. It has spread from
Louisiana into Texas and the surrounding states in the twentieth
century, displacing the older and plainer *peanut* (or *pecan*) *patty.*
Old-fashioned Blacks had used *spreadwide* for the same confection.

Not all the etymologies are as clear. *Chowder* appears to have
been taken from Breton *chaudière,* "cauldron." One of the most
difficult etymological problems is posed by *shanty,* which is
ascribed by some scholars to Canadian French *chantier,* "shed for
storing timber," and by others to Irish *sean,* "old," and *tigh,*
"house." The familiarity of phrases like *shanty Irish* seems to
argue for the latter hypothesis; the nature, place, and dates of the
earliest American citations for the former. The outstanding example of folk etymology among this group of words is *carryall,* a
reworking of *carriole.*

The changes of meaning reflected in the French borrowings are
at times more complex than those from the Amerindians, partly
because so many of the words represent a second borrowing of the
same term. *Portage,* for example, had existed in English for several centuries in a number of meanings, some of which were archaic or obsolescent when the word was borrowed in the present,
highly specialized American sense. *Dime,* with the general meaning of "one-tenth," had come into British English as early as 1377,

but it had dropped out of the language altogether prior to its revival as part of our monetary terminology.

On other occasions the American adoption of a French word
has preceded an independent borrowing in England. For example,
crevasse, which in America refers to a break in a levee, was
adopted some years later in England to indicate a fissure or chasm
in the ice of a glacier. This meaning was subsequently adopted in
America also. The American use of *coulee,* "a small stream or
stream bed," is first cited in 1807, more than thirty years earlier
than the first British borrowing in a technical geological sense, referring to a lava flow.

One of the most interesting series of changes has occurred in
connection with *depot*—pronounced *dee-po* in the South prior to
World War II, but reverting under military influence to something
closer to the French pronunciation. In the late eighteenth century,
it meant the act of depositing, then the deposit or collection itself,
and later a place where virtually anything might be deposited—
military stores, prisoners of war, or merchandise. About 1830,
with the development of the railroad, the term was adopted for "a
goods station at a terminus." In America, however, the term was
extended to freight depositories all along the line and not merely
at terminal points. But also in America, particularly in the sparsely
populated sections of the country where the railroad often pushed
beyond actual settlement, the same small building was regularly
used to store goods, sell tickets, and shelter passengers. Consequently, *depot* came to be used for a passenger station as well.
In about the second decade of the twentieth century, a good deal
of effort was expended in attempting to substitute *station,* often
with such amusing inconsistencies as having the Pennsylvania
Railroad Station located on Depot Street. *Depot* came into its own
again in connection with transcontinental bus travel, but it never
caught on at all with air travel and *bus terminal* is perhaps more
"modern" than *bus depot. Depot wagon,* used as early as 1908
for a horse-drawn vehicle, became *station wagon* as a result of the
declining prestige of *depot.* It might be noted that the latter

compound is international: *station* is used for *ranch* in Australia, and *ranch wagon* is a term occasionally used in America. No tendency toward the reinstatement of *depot wagon* has ever been observed.

Picayune, originally the name of a small coin, has been extended to anything trifling, and at times to the meaning of contemptible. *Apache* represents a curious instance of what might be called a loan followed by repayment. The French, after experimenting with various Indian tribal names as a term for the gangsters in and about Paris, finally hit upon *Apache,* which seemed to be satisfactory. It was then taken back into both British and American English, particularly with reference to the somewhat abandoned type of dancing characteristic of the low-class French halls and cafés. Except for *sashay,* which the *Oxford English Dictionary* with rather unnecessary severity classifies as "U.S. vulgar," the French loan words were all borrowed as nouns. The three in particular which have attained the widest use as verbs are *portage, cache,* and *toboggan.* With the last two the transformation was very rapid, occurring within a quarter of a century after the adoption of the substantive. The same rapidity of conversion may be observed in the change of *picayune* from noun to adjective.

With respect to compound formations, undoubtedly the most prolific of the borrowed words are *prairie,* which is represented by more than eighty combinations. *Gopher,* with fourteen on record makes a poor second, perhaps, but there is a typically American bit of verbal humor in its figurative uses. Free matches at cheap restaurants were once *gophers*—ones that the customers were allowed to "go for." Later, the meaning developed of a person, usually young, employed as a gopher—to "go for" coffee, "go for" cigarettes, etc. Such derivatives as *picayunish, picayunishness, tobogganer,* and *tobogganist* serve to increase the total impact of French upon written English, but pale into insignificance in comparison with the recent popularity of the *-ee* suffix. Particularly striking has been the tendency to apply the originally feminine form of the past participle (-*ée*) to masculine derivatives as well. British English, in general, preserves, or at least used to preserve, the niceties of both gender and written accentuation, but in the United States an *employee* could be either male or female from the time of the first use of that word. World War II saw the popularity of *draftee* and its euphemism *selectee*. Others from about the same time include *rushee, parolee,* and *trainee; conferee* was a very early formation on that model; *escapee,* a recent one, with the derivative ending altered from that of object to subject, as in the case of the even more recent *retiree*—or, for that matter, the somewhat older *divorcee*.

III Spanish Influence

Contact with Spanish explorers began as early as the days when America was still thought of as the "Indies" and when the Caribbean was the Spanish Main. Territories as important to British economic and population expansion as Jamaica and Texas belonged first to Spain, and significant interaction with Spanish speakers has continued from the earliest days of British exploration to the present time.

Moving southward toward the Gulf of Mexico and westward toward the Rockies, the Anglo-Saxon settlers encountered permanent and substantial Spanish colonies in which large individual haciendas subsisted as independent units. The hacienda culture remained important in Mexico until the first decade of the present century. Zebulon Pike, who in 1806 attempted to ascend the peak which now bears his name, Stephen Austin, and Samuel Houston entered into full contact with that culture, as did the intrepid "forty-niners" who crowded into California in 1849 in their frenzied search for gold. The American cowboy learned his trade from the Mexican.

The words still common in American English which may be traced to the Spanish in America, classified according to the aspects of life and fields of activity they represent, are as follows:

Plants and Animals

alfalfa
marijuana
mesquite
yucca
armadillo
bronco
burro
barracuda
bonito
pompano

chigger (jigger)
cockroach
coyote
mustang
palomino
pinto
vinegarroon

Food and Drink

chile con carne
enchilada
frijole
jerk (jerked meat)
mescal
pinion nuts
taco
tamale
tequila
tortilla

Clothing

chaps
poncho
serape
sombrero
ten-gallon hat

Ranch Life

buckaroo
chaparral
cinch
corral
cuarta
hacienda
lariat
lasso
peon
quirt
ranch
reata
rodeo
stampede
wrangler

Building

adobe
cafeteria
patio
plaza
pueblo

Mining

bonanza
placer

Legal and Penal

calaboose
cuartel
desperado
hoosegow
incommunicado
vigilantes

Toponymics

arroyo
barranca
canyon
key
mesa
sierra

Races and Nationalities

conch
coon
creole
dago
mulatto
octoroon
pickaninny
quadroon

Miscellaneous

coquina
fiesta
filibuster
hombre
loco
marina
mosey
pronto
rumba
savvy
stevedore
temblor
tornado
vamoose

The eighty-odd terms listed here, though certainly not all-inclusive, are greater in number than either the borrowings from the various Indian languages or those from the French. And here again is the problem of what to include and what to omit. *Pickaninny, savvy,* and possibly *lasso* have more probable origins in Portuguese (a special variety of which was very important to the multilingual contact situations of the sixteenth, seventeenth, eighteenth and even nineteenth centuries), than in Spanish in the narrowest sense. A class of words with -*oo* (*vamoose, buckaroo*) runs counter to the usual American English treatment of Spanish -*o* (as in *rodeo* and *bronco*), as does a class in -*oon* (*vinegarroon, quadroon, octoroon*). These are first attested from the buffer area between French Louisiana and Spanish Texas, where there is some evidence otherwise of a special Romance contact language. The South Texas (Mexican border) word *mott,* "a clump of trees," is often derived from *mata,* but it poses problems about the dropping of the final vowel, as do *quirt, ranch,* and a few others.

There is always the problem that certain words, like *taco* and *frijole* (from Spanish *frijol,* with a final vowel as a back formation from the plural *frijoles*) are better known along the Mexican border than anywhere else. (*Taco* and *enchilada* were, however, given nationwide spread in the 1970's by fast food restaurants, and even *sopapillos* are becoming commercially well-known.) Others, like *reata,* are widely current only in the Far West, and *palomino* is known mainly to horse fanciers elsewhere. Some fish names, notably *pompano,* are characteristic chiefly of the Gulf Coast. Terms like *alcalde* and *cuartel* are used only in the completely Hispanized sections of New Mexico and Texas. It would be snobbish to leave out *amigo* and *hombre,* popularized by the same Western movies and pulp novels that gave the entire nation *vamoose.*

Still another difficulty arises in connection with certain words. Although such terms as *alligator, avocado, banana, palmetto,* and *potato* were originally Spanish-American in origin, they have become current in British as well as in American English. This is also true of such originally indigenous words as *chocolate* and *tapioca,* the latter in fact having come into American English through Portuguese. It is scarcely justifiable, therefore, to consider these as peculiarly American.

It is immediately obvious that the largest group of adoptions from the Spanish reflects the hacienda culture which typified the Spanish colonial occupation and the ranching and mining economies which developed out of it. There were several stages of that exposure, and the different circumstances of borrowing reflect those differences. The borrowings of the early stages (*wrangler* from *caballerangero, mustang* from *mesteño* or a still unidentified Spanish word, *lariat* from *la reata*) have undergone extreme phonological alteration—much more so than should be expected of borrowings between two languages like Spanish and English with a long history of contact. Later borrowings (*bronco, burro, rodeo, pinto, palomino, sombrero*) seem to represent a period of genuine bilingualism. In the latter part of the nineteenth century, only food names (*tortilla, enchilada, taco*) were borrowed by English. In a long period of English aloofness from Spanish borrowing, food names like *nachos* (believed along the Texas border to be the plural of the nickname of a certain Ignacio, who improvised that dish for some tourists) continued to come into Southwestern English. *Chicano,* possibly a casual-style pronunciation of *Mexicano,* has been borrowed in very recent years to refer to the Southwestern U.S. native of Mexican parentage. *Macho,* meaning "masculine, virile," was generally adopted in the 1970's, and there is even a variant of *hamburger* called *Machoburger. Machismo,* the related abstract noun, is often used by the women's liberation movement as an expression of the dominant quality of a "male chauvinist pig."

As with the French loan words, there is evidence of Spanish borrowing from the languages of the various Indian nations with which they came into contact, prior to the adoption of these words into English. *Coyote* was taken by the Spaniards from Aztec or Nahuatl *coyotl. Tequila* may even have been a Nahuatl borrowing from some other Indian language, and *jerk,* "to preserve," as it occurs in *jerked meat* reflects a Spanish *charquear, charqui,* taken from one of the Peruvian Indian languages. The precise path of transmission of *pickaninny* is, as stated earlier, questionable, as is that of *filibuster.* The last represents Spanish *filibustero* ultimately derived from Dutch *vrijbuiter,* "freebooter." The peculiar phonology suggests some intermediate language of transmission. *Rumba* may have been African before it became Spanish.

English in general borrowed heavily from Spanish, which preceded it during the exploitation of the West Indies and the Americas, in the eighteenth century. Prominent among those early adoptions are such words as *tomato, barbecue, savannah, chocolate,* and *sarsaparilla,* not included in the foregoing lists because they became equally common in Britain and America. Such borrowings also include *cannibal* (and probably *Caliban,* in Shakespeare's *The Tempest*) from the same Carib-Indian word that gave Europe Caribbean (and *Caribe*), and its forms in the various languages.

If variation in phonetic shape is striking, particularly in those borrowings that represent the early learning of the cattle trade by the Anglo-Saxons, no striking deviations from etymological meaning are to be found among these words, although *dago* was presumably derived from the proper name *Diego,* the Spanish equivalent of James. The most picturesque development among all the Spanish borrowing is again an instance of folk or popular etymology. The Spanish word for braid is *galón.* It appears that the wide-brimmed hats worn by cowboys and ranchers were originally decorated with a number of braids at the base of the crown, from which the expression *ten-* (or *five-*) *gallon hat* was derived. This was mistakenly interpreted as a reference to its potential liquid capacity. Beside this, *cockroach,* another attempt to break up a strange word (*cucaracha*) into meaningful elements, appears as a rather inept display of the imagination.

Among the words presenting the most extensive and complex series of meaning changes is *creole.* In the Spanish colonies *criollo* was a term applied to someone born in the region but of European, usually Spanish, ancestry. Naturally enough the word had this meaning in Louisiana when that territory passed from Spanish to French control. The word was taken over by the French and in its French form came to be used for a person born in Louisiana, but of French ancestry. After the American occupation of the area, the term was applied to the dialect of French spoken there, to those who spoke it (consequently at times to persons of mixed French and African ancestry), to native-born as distinguished from African-born Negroes, and to a sauce typical of the cookery of the region. A certain group of linguists uses it—as did Francis Moore in his *Travels in the Inland Parts of Africa* in 1732—to refer to a language like Haitian Creole (or the similar French Creole of Louisiana and many other areas) or Sranan Tongo, an English-based "mixed" language of Suriname.

Some of the concomitant aspects of word borrowing have been discussed in sufficient detail in connection with the Indian and the French loan words so that they need only brief mention here.

Again, most of the Spanish borrowings are nouns, although the adjective *loco,* the adverb *pronto,* and the verbs *vamoose, mosey,* and *savvy* (all of which are, incidentally, on the suspect list insofar as uncomplicated Spanish transmission is concerned) do demonstrate for the first time an influence somewhat deeper than the casual level. Such nouns as *stampede, lasso, ranch, barbecue,* and the hybrids *filibuster* and *jerk* quite readily developed into verbs. *Ranch* has given rise to about a dozen compound forms, and no less than twenty compounds peculiar to American usage have been formed from the noun *mosquito,* even though the word itself appears at times in British as well as in American English.

The most interesting combinative development is to be seen in connection with *cafeteria.* The word appears to have been used around 1908–18 in California, and considerably earlier in Chicago, in its present meaning "self-service restaurant." The Spanish equivalent, however, was recorded in a dictionary of Cuban Spanish published in 1862.

In Spanish, *-ería* was and still is a highly productive suffix. Any Spanish-speaking village or city will be lined with signs bearing such legends as *carnicería* (butcher shop), *ferretería* (hardware store), *planchadería* (clothes pressing), *tintorería* (dry-cleaning or dyeing), *carpentería* (carpenter shop)—and as one approaches the United States border with Mexico, or in Puerto Rico, *lonchería* and *drogería. Cafetería* was merely another formation of this type. The mid-century records of its use in Cuba and Mexico show it to have been applied to a small restaurant serving not only coffee (*café*) but also ordinary alcoholic drinks and plain meals. From here it seems to have spread to the Spanish-speaking residents of California, but as a place for drinking rather than eating. Then, during the last decade of the nineteenth century, it came to be used for a self-service restaurant. Since English already used *café* for a restaurant in which table service was provided, it was natural that the suffix *teria* should be abstracted to mean "self-service." By natural extension a long list including *groceteria, bookateria, snacketeria, hardware-ateria, shaveteria, smoketeria* and *valeteria* developed. Even *coffee-teria* had a temporary vogue. All these, however, have become obsolete in the last decade or so. *Washateria,* for example, is now *laundromat* almost everywhere except in an area of the South which includes Houston, Texas. *Cafeteria* is still much in evidence, but more pretentious self-service may now be called *buffet* or (even less accurately) *smorgasbord.*

IV Dutch Influence

Long before their drive westward had penetrated into the realm of the French *voyageurs* and *habitants* and the Spanish *haciendados,* the aggressive English colonists had dispossessed another European nation of its North American territory—forcibly "trading" the rather unpromising territory that is now Suriname (formerly Dutch Guiana) for New York and the best harbor in the New World. That country was, of course, Holland. Its industrious burghers and powerful patroons became a part of the English colonial empire, in the trade referred to above, in 1664, but its sailors had been in contact with New World–bound Englishmen for a long time before that.

Even during its short existence as part of the far-flung empire of the House of Orange, the settlement in the Hudson Valley had developed a mode of life and a culture quite its own. The virtues of patriarchal home and fireside were mixed with typically New World vices like slavery. (Even so well-known a figure in the struggle for Emancipation as Sojournor Truth began her life as the slave of a New York Dutch family.) This was the world of Walter the Doubter, William the Testy, and hard-headed Peter Stuyvesant, known to many mainly through Washington Irving's *Knickerbocker History.* Caricature though his account may be, Irving does give us a picture of the general culture of the area. However, we should not allow his familiar, comfortable description of cozy uniformity make us forget that Walloons, French Huguenots, and

even contact with Swedish settlements along the Delaware complicated the linguistic picture before the arrival of the British.

The words in the following list are, in some sense, of Dutch origin or show other evidence of Dutch influence, classified according
to the domains which they represent:

Food

cole slaw
cookie
cruller
pit ("stone" or "seed")
pot cheese
waffle

Toponymics

bush ("back country")
hook (of land)

Transportation

caboose
scow
sleigh
span (of horses)

Farm and Building

hay barrack
stoop ("porch")
saw buck

Social Classification

boss
patroon
Yankee

Miscellaneous

boodle
dingus
dope
dumb ("stupid")
logy
poppycock
Santa Claus
snoop
spook

Although only twenty-seven words appear in the list, they are in
much more general use than either the Spanish or the French loan
words. They form a part of the most intimate fabric of American
usage. Six of them pertain to foods, but aside from these there are
few which represent any particular class of idea or sphere of activity.

Some of the terms are wholly or in part translations rather than
direct appropriations from the Dutch lexicon. *Pot cheese* is mod-

eled on Dutch *pot kees. Saw buck* could have been formed either on the basis of Dutch *zaagbock* or German *Sägebock;* the fact that a low German contact language existed in the maritime trade, used by sailors who didn't really care what their language was officially named, may be relevant here. An even stronger case for language-contact origins can be made for *Yankee,* for which Dutch *Jan Kees* ("John Cheese"), is only one possibility. This explanation involves the mistaking of *Kees* for a plural by the English-speaking colonists, and back formation making a new singular *Yankee* (just as, earlier, English had developed the singular *pea* by back formation from *pease*). Another suggestion is that it was a Pidgin English pronunciation of *English;* there are also possible influences from some unflattering words in the Indian languages. We know that the Dutch, then as now, were accomplished sailors and polyglots, and we are not surprised, therefore, to find linguistic complexity in our borrowings from that language.

Since contact with the Dutch colonists was established during the seventeenth century, dictionary citations for approximately one-third of the Dutch loan words have dates prior to 1800. The earliest words to appear in American English were *scow* in 1660, *sleigh* in 1703, *patroon* in 1744, *caboose* in 1747, *stoop* in 1775, and *span* in 1769. Most of the remaining words are found sometime during the first part of the nineteenth century. This is important, for it definitely marks the original settlements in New York as the place of origin of the Dutch borrowings rather than such later colonies as that of the Van Raalte group, which settled in western Michigan in the 1840's, or the subsequent settlements in Wisconsin and Iowa. Moreover, a number of terms of Dutch origin, such as *erve,* "small inheritance," *kolf baan,* "mall for a game played with mallet and ball," *rolliche,* "meat roulade," and *olicook,* "fat cake" (somewhat like a doughnut), are either entirely obsolete or are disappearing rapidly.

There are relatively few major changes in form and pronunciation in the Dutch borrowings. Such folk etymologies as exist are those that convert place names like *Hellegat,* "bright gate," to

Hell Gate and *Crummaslue* to *Gramercy Park*. A good many of the words now spelled with *oo*, some of which are pronounced with the vowel of *food*, were spelled *oe* in Dutch and pronounced with the vowel of *pull*. This was true of *hoek, snoepen,* and *stoep,* corresponding to English *hook, snoop,* and *stoop,* respectively. *Claus,* in *Santa Claus,* developed from a Dutch *Sinterklaas,* a somewhat collapsed form of Sant Nikolaas. However, since the variety of American English through which the borrowings took place apparently did not have the [a] vowel of *father,* the [ɔ] vowel, as in *log,* developed as the closest approximation. This is also true of *boss* (Dutch *baas*).

Undoubtedly the word *caboose* presents the most unusual example of a change from its original meaning. At the outset, it was used with reference to a ship's galley, and is still so employed in Great Britain. Subsequent American meanings, however, include that of outdoor oven (1786), hut (1839), and finally its present meaning of a car serving as the headquarters for a freight train crew. (Earlier citations for this meaning have *caboose car.*) In the wagon trains which carried the pioneers westward, the *caboose* was the wagon set aside for provisions. The reference to railroading is first attested in 1871, and of course the wagon trains themselves were soon afterward completely obsolete.

The word *boss* has an interesting cultural as well as phonological history. In Black American English, as is well known, it is an adjective meaning "superlative": a *boss chick* is a really "fine" girl. The same usage is to be observed, as might be expected, in Sranan Tongo, the English Creole of Suriname, where some Dutch slaveowners moved after the British takeover of New York. James Fenimore Cooper, in *The American Democrat* (1838), explained the use of the noun form as a rejection, by white domestic servants, of *master* (probably "Massa"), the form of address used by Black slaves when they were servants. Whether Cooper was right or not—and many of his hypotheses about American English origins are intriguing but perhaps unprovable—a polyglot, multiracial influence in the spread of *boss* seems likely.

We must also recognize that a number of words took only one meaning from the language of the Low Countries, but have other meanings which already existed in English. This is true, for example, of *pit,* in the sense of the hard kernel of a peach or cherry. It is only this one particular use which was borrowed from Dutch; other meanings of this extremely familiar word were already common to both languages. (All of these meanings may have contributed to a slang expression of the 1970's, "It's the pits"—meaning it's about as bad as it could be.) Other instances of the same process include *bush,* with the meaning of back country, *stoop* for porch, and *span* used with reference to horses. It should be observed that the distribution of some of these meanings, such as *pit* and *stoop,* as well as of certain whole word borrowings, is distinctly regional. *Hay barrack* is definitely confined to the Hudson Valley—and to those residents thereof thoroughly familiar with farming—and *pot cheese* is limited to a slightly larger area which includes eastern Pennsylvania and northern New Jersey as well. The commercial term *cottage cheese* is, as elsewhere, a strong competitor to the regional term.

Except for the adjective *dumb* in the sense of "stupid" (which could also reflect some German influence)—the word has a long history in English in the meaning of "silent"—and the verb *snoop,* most of the Dutch loan words were borrowed as nouns, but they lent themselves easily to change of functions. *Pit, boss,* and *sleigh* were all changed into verbs. *Boodle,* perhaps, presents the outstanding illustration of the tendency to form derivatives. The *Oxford English Dictionary* lists *boodleize, boodleism, boodleistic, boodler, boodlerism,* and *boodling,* and the *Dictionary of Americanisms* adds *boodlery* to the list. None of these is in widely current usage in the 1980's.

V The German Influence

The German element in the vocabulary of American English is the first, among those considered, to stem from an immigrant people, not a conquered colonial rival. It is also the first for which no special contact variety, pidgin or otherwise, is known—at least, during this early period. Unlike Dutch, Spanish, and French, German was not encountered to any great extent in the West Indies or at sea. These factors give a somewhat different turn to the word-borrowing process.

The German migrations to America consist of three or four major waves. As early as 1683, immigrants from the southwestern part of Germany had begun to settle in Pennsylvania. By 1775 they numbered about 90,000, largely from the Rhenish Palatinate. These Germans developed a language consisting of a compromise of their own various dialects with a strong admixture of English words and constructions. We have come to know and refer to this as Pennsylvania Dutch (from *Deutsch*). Though dying out more rapidly now than in former times, it is still spoken by about 25 per cent of the inhabitants of Lehigh, Lebanon, and Berks counties in Pennsylvania, and understood by 60 to 65 per cent. Its extraordinary persistence is due to the clannishness of the Pennsylvania Germans, based in part upon the religious separatism evident in such sects as the Amish and the Mennonites. The English of these Pennsylvania Germans has its own very distinctive flavor, expressed in perhaps stereotyped examples like "The pants are too tight; I'll have to leave [German *lassen*] out the seat," and "Throw your father down the stairs his hat."

The second wave of German migration began as early as 1830, but reached its crest in 1849, after the collapse of the liberal movement in the fatherland, when such patriots as Carl Schurz came to this country. Although many German rural communities sprang up as a result of the movement, much of the settlement was metropolitan. In Milwaukee, Chicago, Cleveland, Cincinnati, St. Louis, Detroit, Buffalo, and New York, Germans were gathered together in groups large enough to maintain their own language and cultural traditions for a considerable length of time. German-language dailies flourished in all the large cities of the Middle West until 1917. The Germans had their own schools as well, and they maintained strong church and fraternal organizations. Subsequent large-scale movements in the 'eighties of the last century and early in the present century tended to maintain the traditions of the fatherland for a considerable period of time. Despite the curtailment of immigration under the quota system after the First World War, the Germans still constitute the largest body of non-English-speaking stock in the United States, with the possible exception of Spanish-speaking Chicanos, Puerto Ricans, and Cubans.

The words in American English which are of German origin or show some aspects of German influence, classified according to domains, are:

Food and Drink

beer soup
blutwurst
bock beer
delicatessen
dunk
fossnocks
frankfurter
hamburger
lager beer
liverwurst
noodle
ponhaus
pretzel
pumpernickel
sauerbraten
sauerkraut
schnitzel
smear case
snits
springerle
stollen
sweitzer cheese
thick milk
wienerwurst
zwieback

Educational

diener ("laboratory assistant")
festschrift
semester
seminar

Social

Belschnickel
beer garden
bower ("jack" or "knave")
Christmas tree

Social

Kris Kringle
pinochle
rathskeller

saengerfest	fresh ("impudent")
stein	hausfrau
Turner	hex (noun and verb)
turnverein	katzenjammer
	loafer
Miscellaneous	nix
	phooey
bub	spiel, spieler
bum	wunderkind

The loan words listed here are about fifty in number, but again there is the difficulty of knowing what to include and what to omit. Should *turnverein* be considered in current use, or are the gymnastic, literary, and recreational organizations founded through the impetus given by Vater Jahn now completely a dead letter in American life? Or if *turnverein* is obsolescent, how about *Turners,* or *Turner Hall,* which may linger on somewhat more tenaciously? And the *saengerfeste,* though not as numerous as they once were, still survive in various parts of the country, as for example the region around New Braunfels, Texas. Terms like these have been included, not because they are known to the great majority of American English speakers, but in order to give a picture of the historical influence of German comparable to that of the other languages discussed.

Then there is the problem of such compounds as *rainworm, cookbook,* and *back country,* which may be explained as translations of *Regenwurm, Kockbuch,* and *Hinterland* respectively; but they could conceivably have arisen as purely native developments. Even Superman, the truly unique product of modern comic-book culture, might be reckoned to have his origin ultimately in Nietzsche; if so, then the new comic strip "Superheroes," with all the supernaturally strong characters spawned in imitation of Clark Kent's *alter ego* must reflect the same influence at another remove.

Regionally distributed terms occasionally trace back to languages, like German, widely spoken in the area. In this case, examples are *ponhaus*, "scrapple," *fossnocks*, "doughnuts," and *Belschnickel*, "Santa Claus," current chiefly in the Pennsylvania Dutch and derivative areas.

Numerous German words that became a part of the everyday vocabulary during World War II have been omitted mainly because they were equally or more widely used in England. There is also the factor that *Blitzkrieg* ("lightning warfare," applied especially to Hitler's rapid conquest of France), and its shortened form Blitz; *Flak* ("anti-aircraft guns or the fire therefrom," from *Fliegerabwehre Kanone*); *Luftwaffe*, "Air Force"; *Panzer*, "armored division"; and Gestapo, "secret police" have disappeared along with German military might. *Lebensraum*, the need of the German nation for more space, and *German-American Bund* were constantly in the daily papers in the 1940's, but they may be virtually unknown in the 1980's.

Despite these difficulties, the list of German borrowings gives us an idea of the cultural contact between German immigrants and their English-speaking hosts. There can be little doubt that a considerable portion of this contact centered on the dining room table, the free-lunch counter (when there were such things!), and the tavern bar. There is a decided persistence of food terms and words reflecting pleasant but commonplace social contacts. In contrast, the educational terms reflect not so much the German migration to America as the nineteenth-century practice of American educators and professional men to travel to Germany for postgraduate study. The American academic community shares with that of England the use of terms like *Zeitgeist, Vorlage* (at least for philologists), and *Festschrift*. The impact upon the American educational system is, in fact, considerably more profound than these few terms would indicate, since it includes such features as the elective system of courses, the ideal of academic freedom, and the current concept of study leading to the doctorate.

In general, the German borrowings came into English during the nineteenth century. Although both *noodle*, first cited by the *Dictionary of American English* in 1812, and *sauerkraut*, in 1813, seem to have been used in England considerably earlier, there is every reason to believe that the American use of these words represents an independent borrowing. These, along with *Kris Kringle* in 1830, *loafer* in 1835, *poker* in 1836, and *ouch* in 1839, must have come from Pennsylvania or its derivative settlements. They are certainly too early for the nineteenth-century migrations centering about the 'forty-eighters to have taken effect. The earliest citation dates for the remaining words are distributed fairly evenly throughout the century. Even such commonplaces of present-day American life as *pretzel, hamburger,* and *frankfurter* do not put in their appearance until 1874, 1884, and 1899 respectively. In general the German borrowings have been nouns, but it is of some interest to observe such interjections as *nix, ouch,* and *phooey*— some of which could also have been Yiddish—among them, and it has been assumed that *hurrah* was an early importation from the German as well. Words of this nature indicate something deeper than most casual linguistic intercourse.

Probably the most productive word-forming elements accruing from this contact with the German language are the prefix *ker-* and the suffixes *-fest* and *-burger*. The first of these, possibly traceable to the German past-participle prefix *ge-,* appears chiefly in such colloquial combinations as *kerflop, kerplunk, kersmash.* We find *-fest* in *gabfest, talkfest, swatfest,* and *slugfest.* It is *-burger,* however, which presents by far the most interesting series of developments.

Frankfurter, wienerwurst, braunschweiger, and *thüringer* are, like *Hamburger steak,* types of meat labeled in terms of their presumed place of origin. The last is attested first in 1884 but shortened to *hamburger* by 1901. This word was then transferred to the sandwich made by serving fried ground beef in a bun. *Hamburger steak* continues to be served as a distinct, and more expensive, item on many menus; *chopped steak* (or *chopped sirloin*) is slowly replacing it. Since the element *ham-* was identical to an English word—although the ingredient of the sandwich was not identical to its referent—*burger* came to be used for all the nonmeat elements. It was quite possible to simply order "a burger." As the filling element of the sandwich varied, for the less restricted but still not sophisticated palate of the post-depression era, lunch counters and drive-in restaurant menus began to feature *cheeseburgers, chicken-* (or *chick-*) *burgers, turkeyburgers, lamburgers, ham-and-egg burgers* (there was a prevalent joke, "We got one made out of ham, too, but we don't know what to call it."), *riceburgers, fishburgers, shrimpburgers, pizzaburgers*—in fact there were some thirty, including *turtleburgers* and *rabbitburgers*. *Wimpyburger* celebrated a character in the comic strip "Popeye" who was always begging for hamburgers. Of these, only *cheeseburger* and *hamburger* remain in general usage. The fast food chains proliferate fancy names (*Whopper, Big Mac, Quarterpounder*) for the beef-filled bun, and more pretentious designations like *filet of fish* replace *fishburger*.

Onions were an important ingredient of the taste of the hamburger, but some customers, especially women, asked the short-order cook to "hold the onions." The result was sometimes called a *sissyburger*. The opposite may or may not be what is now referred to as a *macho burger*, with the hybrid use of a newly popular borrowing from Spanish, with the meaning "he man." The mid-1970's saw the development of *Hamburger Helper*, a brand name which threatens to become a common noun designating the way a poor man ekes out a meal by adding filler to the once-cheap ground beef.

Some of the borrowed German words mentioned above could have come more directly from Yiddish; in fact, they quite possibly can be traced to German in one area and to Yiddish in another. Yiddish loans are especially widespread in metropolitan areas: *gefilte fish, schlemihl, schmuck, schnook, shickse, yenta,* and *kibitzer* are generally well known. Since Yiddish has been the home language of many radio and television comedians, as well as that of advertising copywriters, many Yiddish turns of phrase ("Mink, schmink! So long as it keeps you warm!" "I should have stood in bed." "It shouldn't happen to a dog!" "With friends like you, who needs enemies?" and "For this I drove five miles!") have become part of at least the passive repertory of American expressions.

Other immigrant groups have also enriched the English of America. The contribution of the African-derived slaves is only beginning to be appreciated. For a long time, it was known that such individual words as *gumbo, goober, buckra, jazz, juba, voodoo* (or *hoodoo*), *okra, pojo* (a heron, made by folk etymology into "Po' Joe"), and possibly *chigger* were Africanisms. Familiarity with the conjure vocabulary yields *mojo* or *mojo hand* (often shortened to *hand*) and many adaptations of native English words, like *doctor* for "voodoo practitioner." David Dalby of the London School of Oriental and African Studies has, on the other hand, pointed out that many Black American expressions like *be with it, do your thing,* and *bad mouth* (talk badly about someone) are word-for-word translations of phrases used widely in West African languages. Special compounding of English words according to Black and Afro-Caribbean patterns exist in *cut-eye,* "an expression of contempt," and *suck-teeth,* "an expression of insubordination." No etymological suggestion in recent years has aroused such a furor as Dalby's tracing of the most familiar Americanism of them all, *O.K.,* to a group of expressions in West African languages resembling the Wolof words *waw kay.* Nevertheless, it makes more sense than the accepted etymology of a playful acronym from *oll korrect.*

Africanisms in American English tend to have been "masked," in the sense intended by the great anthropologist Melville J. Herskovits, behind familiar words. The Wolof word *hipikat,* "one who has his eyes open, is aware" seems to have given us the musical and street slang uses of *hip,* as well as *cat* meaning "a person." Slight distortions by whites produced things like *hepcat,* in the swing era of the 1930's, "one who enjoyed really up-to-date jazz." Black street slang, spreading from jazz and rock-and-roll musicians to teenagers in the United States and all over the world, popularized many of these words and expressions on an international level.

Lorenzo Dow Turner's *Africanisms in the Gullah Dialect* (1949) suggested that as many as 6,000 African words may have survived on the islands off the coast of North Carolina, South Carolina, and Georgia. More recent work on the Black English vernacular shows the ancestor Plantation Creole to have been spoken wherever there were large numbers of slaves—including the Northern states in the eighteenth century and Nova Scotia—and explains the Gullah Africanisms as survivals, rather than as purely local developments.

If, as several researchers on the subject insistently maintain, Black English and American Indian Pidgin English have their origins in the Pidgin English language contact tradition of the colonial period, they have a fellow in Hawaii—Hawaiian Pidgin (or Creole) English. Partly through this medium, the relatively new state in the Pacific has added a number of words from the native Polynesian language. *Kane* "man," *wahine* "girl," *hula, lei, aloha,* and a smattering of other words have long been fairly well known in the continental United States, partly because of Tin Pan Alley adaptations of Hawaiian music. Sailors, particularly during World War II, became familiar with a number of others, like *poi.* On the Hawaiian islands themselves, mainlanders by birth join the polyglot and polynational population in using a certain amount of Pidgin, and in sprinkling their English with a certain number of Hawaiian words and phrases: *kaukau* "eat" (related to Chinese Pidgin English *chow* and *chow chow*), *pahoehoe* "lava," *luau* (untranslatable, but about halfway between a feast and a party), *mahalo* "thank you," *wikiwiki* "quickly," *pau* "finished or ended," and many others. For most citizens of the continental forty-nine states working in Hawaii, the learning of Hawaiian is relatively superficial; but many an office in Honolulu closes to the words *Pau Hana* ("Work finished").

In addition, languages as widely varied as Swedish, Italian, and

Chinese have all made contributions to the American vocabulary. Owing to the numbers of Scandinavian restaurants which have become established throughout the country, the institution and the term smorgasbord is familiar to millions of Americans. (The term, often misapplied to any kind of self-service restaurant, has given rise to hybrids like *Chinese Smorgasbord.*) *Lutfisk, skijor,* and *skijoring* are well known in those regions originally settled by Swedes and Norwegians. Italian is represented by food terms like *spaghetti, ravioli, minestroni, spumone, tutti frutti,* and *pizza. Pizzeria* has not caught on so well; some Americans apparently think of it as the Italian version of *pissoir,* and an occasional provincial restaurant announces itself as a *Pizza-ria.* The Chinese, from a background of speaking many different varieties and often using Pidgin English even among themselves, have added *chow, chow mein, chop suey, fantan,* and *joss*—the last especially in the combination *joss house* "temple," which is included in the tour of Chinatown in almost any large city. Chinese and other varieties of Pidgin English have contributed a host of expressions like *can do, no can do,* and even the burlesque *no tickee, no laundee.*

In fact, almost every region of the United States heavily populated by one immigrant stock has borrowed a number of words from the foreign language in question, words which generally have a fairly limited local currency. But this situation can change quickly; the term *sauna* for "steambath" was, until about twenty years ago, confined to the northern peninsula of Michigan, where there are large numbers of people of Finnish extraction. In the intervening two decades, it has become a household—and apartment complex—word, owing to the popularity of its use in health clubs and recreational facilities.

Examples could be multiplied indefinitely, but enough has been said to demonstrate that the kinds of words which Americans have borrowed from other languages are not the result of mere whim or chance, but instead bear eloquent testimony to the nature of our contact with the culture that each of those languages represents. "Milestones of general history," is how the Danish scholar

Otto Jespersen once characterized loan words, for, as he said, "they show the course of civilization and the wandering of inventions and institutions, and in many cases give us valuable information as to the inner life of nations." If rightly interpreted, loan words will inform us of the reciprocal relations between peoples.

This chapter has attempted to demonstrate, as well, that there is considerably more to the process of word borrowing than mere addition to the vocabulary; that changes in meaning after the word is taken over, changes in grammatical function, the formation of new compounds, and the isolation of productive word-forming elements are all a part of the process.

At the turn of the present century, Israel Zangwill applied the term *melting pot* to the America which was fast becoming a complex of many old-world cultures. Long before this, Hector St. John Crèvecoeur had recognized that "here individuals of all nations are melted into a new race of men." The melting was never completed, however, and many areas still reflect component elements of a strongly ethnic culture. The distinctive American vocabulary was in great part formed through the acquisition of words, phrases, and idioms from the many languages and cultures represented historically in our population.

4
Colonial Lag and Leveling

So far we have considered the words which came into the English language as a result of its extension to the New World. These words, with a few minor exceptions, had not been in the language at all before. They can be accounted for chiefly in terms of the particular social and linguistic contacts peculiar to America. But that is only part of the story of American English. To understand the impact of these and other innovations, we must have some appreciation of the state of the language into which these words were introduced.

We must remind ourselves of two important facts: first, that the colonists who crossed the ocean in the seventeenth century were speaking the language varieties available to them during that period; and second, that languages change with time, but not always in the same way among various groups who speak the language. When speakers from the mother country comment upon their language as spoken in a colony, they are almost always struck by two things: the unprecedented innovations and the unbelievable archaisms of the colonists. This seeming paradox is fairly easily resolved: The visitors are typically struck by whatever is different from their own usage, whether it is old-fashioned or new-fangled.

Eighteenth-century visitors were impressed by the uniformity of the language spoken in North America. Like the immigrant Alexis Tocqueville, they tended to feel that "There is no patois in the New World." John Pickering, along with Noah Webster easily the most distinguished of our early philologists, also remarked on the great uniformity of dialect throughout the United States: "In consequence," as he said, "of the frequent removals of people from one part of our country to another." British travelers even wrote that the Americans, "except the poor slaves," spoke English "of great classical purity." The observation that dialect was less prevalent in America than in England was the most frequent one, especially before 1770.

The feature of apparent archaism has been most conventionally addressed. Sir William Craigie, the original editor of the *Dictionary of American English,* was partly guided by his perception of that feature, and as early as 1850 J. O. Halliwell's *Dictionary of Archaisms and Provincialisms* included words "now obsolete in England, all of which are familiar and in common use in America." About 300 of these were included in the dictionary. The same idea is implicit in the ironic, if not linguistically sophisticated, statement by James Russell Lowell that Americans "unhappily could bring over no English better than Shakespeare's."

Unfortunately, the proponents of the notion of archaism in American English are often vague and superficial in their expositions of it. On an average of once every five years some well-meaning amateur in the field of folklore or cultural history "discovers" that either the Kentucky, Virginian, or Ozark mountaineers, or members of some relatively isolated group, speak the undefiled English of Chaucer or Shakespeare. The evidence adduced usually runs to such stereotyped examples as *ax* for *ask, hit* for *it, mought* for *might,* and *bigged* for "to get with child." Actually it is quite wrong to suppose that any form of American English has preserved the language of the fourteenth or the sixteenth century without any change whatever. However, the impressions of archaism remain to be accounted for.

As in dealing with innovations from other languages, we start with vocabulary. *Loan,* used as a transitive verb, is labeled an Americanism in most dictionaries. British prefers *lend.* Verbal *loan* originated, perhaps as early as 1200, in England; in the form *lonyng* in the papers of Henvy VIII, and in two seventeenth-century citations, the existence of the form is unmistakable. American writings employ *loan* in a verbal function as early as 1729, and indeed all of the *Oxford English Dictionary* citations for the eighteenth century are American sources. For the nineteenth and twentieth centuries, American writers continue to furnish the bulk of evidence for its use, and the 1864 edition of Webster seems to have been the first dictionary to record it.

Greenhorn gives just a slightly different twist to the archaizing process. In the sense of a novice or raw, inexperienced person, the word is not unknown in England but nevertheless is considerably more common in America. The *Oxford English Dictionary* records British citations illustrating this meaning from 1682 on, but whether by accident or design, none later than 1806. A 1790 citation is drawn from a book dealing with the West Indies, an area to which historical linguists have not paid adequate attention for analogues to American English. The nineteenth-century citations are all from American authors. It seems that the word jumped not merely from England to the American mainland but probably to the overseas colonies generally, and then it continued in active use in this country, although no longer current in England.

Another convenient sketch of the same tendency, but this time with a significant addendum, is presented by the *Oxford English Dictionary* on the verb *to progress.* We are told here that the word was common in England from 1590 to 1670, that it became obsolete in England in the eighteenth century but was apparently retained in America, where it became very common toward the end of the century. It was readopted in England after 1800 but often characterized there as an Americanism, and it is still more frequently used in the United States. Evidence of the mid-nineteenth century status of the word in England is furnished by the following quotation from Mary Russell Mitford, writing in *Lights and Shadows of American Life* in 1832: "In country towns . . . society has been progressing (if I may borrow that expressive Americanism) at a very slow rate."

This is the basic pattern which characterizes dozens of so-called archaisms in American English. The particular words behaving in this fashion cannot always be accounted for, but there are certain circumstances in which such a development is likely to take place. First of all, there are situations where British English appears to have acquired two synonymous words for the same thing or idea at about the time of our earliest colonial settlement. One striking illustration of this is afforded by the English equivalents for what we in America call a bedbug. First of all, the word *bug,* originally signifying in England, as it now does in America, an insect of any kind, specialized in meaning and came to be applied only to the offensive little creatures found chiefly in beds and bedsteads. The earliest citation of this special use is 1622.

Borrowed, at almost precisely the same time and in the West Indies as well as the mainland, was the Spanish word *chinche,* "bedbug," in the form *chinch.* Thus, throughout the seventeenth century, *chinch* and *bug* were synonymous in England. After 1700 *chinch* appears scarcely at all in the mother country, but there are increasing indications of its use overseas. A citation dated 1730 suggests that the term was used by Negroes. There is evidence of it in Jamaica in 1756. Of the two nineteenth-century citations in the *Oxford English Dictionary,* one is American; the other is British, but it refers to "the impolite animal which the transatlantics delicately designate a *chintz.*" Of two synonymous words in existence when American settlement began, *bug* remained current in England: *chinch* became archaic. Since the earlier general meaning of *bug* had been brought to America by the first colonists, *chinch* continued in use there for a considerable time as the word for bed-bug, and in fact *chinch-bug* is still widely current.

The word *andiron* seems to tell much the same story. There is evidence of its use in England from 1300 on. But late in the six-teenth century (1596) the compound *firedogs* also came to be applied to the same article and has continued in use down to the present. Hester Piozzi still used *andirons* in 1789, but in 1826 Sir Walter Scott felt it necessary to write, "The andirons or *dogs*—for retaining the blazing firewood on the hearth." Subsequent quota-tions in the *Oxford English Dictionary* are American. *Firedogs* is used in some regions of the United States, but certainly the more common *andirons* must have been brought to this country at a time when the two words were equally current in England.

At other times the creation or acceptance of a new term in En-gland well after the beginnings of colonization resulted in the dis-placement of an older word in the mother country which, how-ever, continued in use in America. This may be illustrated by *druggist*. In the early seventeenth century this term replaced the older *apothecary* which had acquired a somewhat unfavorable meaning. It was used in England as the principal term for a retail seller of medicinal drugs throughout the seventeenth century and the first half of the eighteenth century; it spread also to Scotland and the American colonies. But about 1750 or slightly before, in England itself, either a desire for elegance or for more precise defi-nition appears to have extended the meaning of *chemist* to apply to a retail drug merchant. This extension was so complete that by 1800 *druggist* had virtually disappeared from popular usage, though retained in the combination *chemist-and-druggist* by the terms of various licensing acts. In America and Scotland the older *druggist* simply continued in use.

Frequently, too, the archaic survivals in America, though not current in standard British English, may be found still firmly en-trenched in the English local or regional dialects. For example, with reference to the compound *cordwood*, the *Oxford English*

Dictionary comments, "now chiefly in America," suggesting some currency throughout England at an earlier period. However, the only English citations are one for 1638–9 from the *North Riding Records,* another from a Kentish gloss of 1887, and a third from the 1763 volume of the *British Magazine,* but used with reference to America. The picture which thus emerges is one of regional use in seventeenth-century England, transportation to America where it became a common term, and possibly a weak extension to eighteenth-century standard British English, but certainly one which did not survive for any considerable period of time.

The case for *shoat,* "a young weaned pig," as a word once current in standard British English use is even clearer. Citations, in evidence as early as 1413, are especially numerous throughout the seventeenth century. They continue through 1722. Those appearing for the late eighteenth and early nineteenth centuries, however, are ascribed to Norfolk and Wiltshire respectively. Meanwhile the word was carried to America and has continued in use in the United States down to the present day. *Deck,* for a pack of cards, apparently in common use throughout England in the sixteenth century, survives in England only in the northern dialect but is the normal term in the United States.

Similarly, *cater-cornered* is cited only for Shropshire and Leicester, and other uses of *cater-* as a compounding element are also confined to local dialects. *Drool,* used in America by Thoreau in 1854, appears to be a Somerset word; *squirt,* employed as a personal appellative, is cited from Cheshire; *pond,* for a natural, not an artificial, body of water is employed in Surrey. *Polliwog* seems to have been current throughout England until the middle of the seventeenth century; since then it has receded to the East Anglian and northern counties, although it is widely used in the United States.

The dictionary treatment of the verb *wilt* reveals a fascinating instance of a word originating in the English regional dialects, then having wide adoption in the United States, and subsequently spreading to the standard language in England. Applied originally to plants, it developed in the English north-country, as evidenced by John Ray's dialect collection of 1691. It jumped the ocean in the course of the eighteenth century and developed a figurative or transferred meaning in America: "to become limp, to lose energy or vigor." Nineteenth-century American writers who employed the term include Timothy Dwight, Washington Irving, James Russell Lowell, and John Neal. At the very close of the century it was again picked up by a British writer and in 1920 appears in the *Times Literary Supplement*.

Often it is not the whole semantic range of a word but an archaic or older meaning which survives in American usage, whereas in England subsequent semantic developments have occurred. We have already seen this to be true of *bug,* for which American English preserves the early general meaning, whereas the specialized significance "bedbug" prevails in England today.

A similar development may be observed in connection with the word *sick.* H. W. Fowler, in his *Dictionary of Modern English Usage,* treating the status of the term in England, points out that, "The original and more general sense of *sick,* which has now been transferred for the most part to *ill,* was suffering from any bodily disorder. That sense remains to it in attributive use (*sick people, a sick child,* etc.), but is now uncommon in predicative use (*be, feel sick*), in which it means vomiting or ready to vomit. In U. S. and Scotch use the wider sense is still common. . . ." Actually this specialization appears to have begun early in the seventeenth century, but it was the general rather than the special meaning which was carried to America and which has prevailed there.

The word *apartment* offers another illustration of the same tendency, operating, however, with the aid of the grammatical form and functions of plurality. This term was, from 1641 on, applied to a portion of a house or building consisting of a suite of rooms allotted to the use of a particular family. *Apartment* still has this meaning in the United States. In England, beginning in 1715, *apartment* seems to have been confined in meaning to a single room, the older sense of a suite of rooms being expressed by the term *flat* or by the plural *apartments*. This plural development did not spread to the United States, where single-room quarters must be referred to as *one-room apartments*.

In those cases where America retained the older meaning of a word, the newer British meaning was not always in the direction of greater precision, narrowness, or specialization. Quite as frequently the opposite development occurred, and the word assumed a broader significance in England. For instance, *chemist* was expanded in England to include those who prepared and sold medicinal drugs. Much the same sort of development may be observed in the word *tariff*.

Originally an Arabic word, *tariff* came into English through Italian and referred to an arithmetical table or statement, but was applied almost as early to an official list or schedule setting forth the several customs duties to be imposed on imports or exports. In England, a further extension to include the list of charges at a hotel or restaurant, found as early as 1751, remains today as a common meaning of the word. Ultimately this generalization was also carried to the United States, but only to the extent that we might, in this country, conceivably speak of a hotel or railroad tariff, though we would normally do so only by employing a specifying or limiting term. *Tariff* by itself still means customs duties in the United States.

Not infrequently words acquire, in the course of time, a somewhat different status in England and America. The word *baggage* affords an excellent illustration. It came into the language early in the fifteenth century and meant what is now called *luggage* in England. This meaning has survived as the ordinary term in the United States; it died out in England at the close of the eighteenth century. A special military use, "the portable equipment of the army," continues in England as well as the United States, but in general the most striking English developments were unfavorable. Such meanings as "rubbish," "purulent or corrupt matter," and "trashy article," all appear in sixteenth-century British use. Just a bit later it was applied to a disreputable woman, or strumpet; citations for this range from Shakespeare to William Thackeray. Only a very mild and playful version of this epithet came to America—witness Irving's "a pretty, soft-hearted baggage"—and this is nearly obsolete. But American English has no less than twenty-five combinations for *baggage* meaning "luggage."

A word may begin to change its status by being typed as something other than upper-class speech. This happened to *jack* for *knave* in cards. The ordinary term in the United States is *jack*. The word was first used in this sense in the game of *all fours,* some time in the seventeenth century. A little later it spread for a time to all card games, and apparently it was this broadened meaning that was carried to America. By 1861, however, we find Estella in *Great Expectations* saying with disdain, "He calls the knaves, Jacks, this boy!" and currently it is classified as non-upper-class English speech.

The development of an unfavorable meaning in a word is called pejoration. There are several dramatic instances of such change in British English, occurring in words which have retained their older, relatively neutral significance in the United States. Students of the theater will recall the furor created by George Bernard Shaw when, early in the twentieth century, he had one of the characters in *Pygmalion* use the word *bloody*. No American could possibly appreciate this; the word is quite neutral here, but Mencken has said, "in England it is regarded as indecent, with overtones of the blasphemous." Its history is briefly outlined by the *Oxford English Dictionary* as follows: "In general use from the Restoration to 1750. Now constantly in the mouths of the lowest classes, but by respectable people considered a horrid word." For a while, at least, *stomach* acquired taboo characteristics in England and was avoided in ordinary conversation. None of these pejorative developments have occurred on the American continent, where the words retain their older neutral and unblemished character.

The opposite semantic development, namely where a word in the course of time becomes less objectionable, or even positively more respectable, is called amelioration. This seems to have oc-

curred in England with respect to the word *nasty,* which in its
original sense meant "foul, filthy, dirty." Today it is greatly toned
down, often indicating nothing more than what is somewhat unpleasant or mildly disagreeable. American use is still generally
closer to the earlier meaning.

The word *lobbyist* presents an even more striking instance of
British amelioration, this time of a term which is really American
in origin. It was coined to apply to those who frequent the lobbies
of the national House of Representatives, the Senate, and other
lesser legislative bodies in order to influence members in the exer-
cise of their lawmaking functions. There is in the American use of
the term usually a suggestion of improper influence. When the
word was transferred to England and applied to the House of
Commons it came to refer to a journalist frequenting the lobbies
there for the purpose of picking up items of political interest. So
thoroughly did the ameliorative process operate, and so respectable did the word become, that Mencken cites an instance of a
commemorative tablet in St. Bride's Church, Fleet Street, designating the honored individual as a "Lobbyist in the Palace of West-
minster and London."

Thus far we have been concerned with words retaining older
meanings in America but in which a specific direction of semantic
change is visible in England. In many instances, however, the English simply discontinued employing certain senses of words,
senses which are still current in America. *Fall* for "autumn" is one
of these. Its use began in England in 1545. Now, however, in the
U. S. it is the ordinary term for autumn; in England, it is "now
rare in literary use though found in some dialects," according to
the *Oxford English Dictionary.* It is difficult to find out from the
dictionary evidence just when the term did die out in England, although it seems to have been some time during the second half of
the nineteenth century.

The word *raise* offers another instance of the same tendency. In
England, farm or garden products are grown, animals are bred,
and children are reared; in America, all of them are raised.

Curiously enough, *raise* was once used in all these senses in England. These extensions of meaning seem to have occurred in the seventeenth and eighteenth centuries, at which time they were transported westward, and though soon dying out in England, gained strength and became a permanent fixture of the language of the Americans.

There are further illustrations. The verb *clod* as applied to soils occurred in British use from 1530 to 1741, but the meaning is still current in America. *Quit,* in the sense of "to stop," does not continue in England after 1754. *Cabin,* now confined to nautical use in England, meant "a poor dwelling" up to 1832. If nothing else, the title of Harriet Beecher Stowe's famous work has served to perpetuate the word *cabin* in the United States.

In the general area of pronunciation, the American variety of English is equally notable for its perpetuation of older features of the language. This is true, for example, of the two sounds which offer the most marked difference between British English, at least of the south-country variety, and the language spoken by the majority of Americans: namely, the vowels of *fast, bath, calf,* and *aunt* on the one hand, and those of *earth, turn, firm,* and *word* on the other.

The words in the first group are pronounced in what historian of English H. C. Wyld and phonetician Daniel Jones have termed Received Standard [British] English with the stressed vowel of *father,* and generally in American English with the vowel of *cat.* (A notable exception is the Black speaker, who, even in the deepest South, pronounces *aunt*—most usually *aunty*—with the vowel that Americans consider "British" in that word.) It is believed that *fast, calf,* and *bath* were pronounced in England of the sixteenth century as they are in America today. There is some disagreement over the precise way in which and the time in which the broad [ɑ] developed, but there is reason to believe that even as late as the mid-eighteenth century it had not yet been adopted. Sheridan's pronouncing dictionary, published in 1780, gives no indication of the existence of an [ɑ] vowel in England for words of this group.

An Orthoepic Analysis of the English Language by T. Batchelor, as late as 1809, is likewise lacking in such evidence. On the American side of the ocean, the vowel of *cat*, [æ], appears even for words like *father* and *hardly* in the phonetic alphabet devised in 1768 by that versatile genius, Benjamin Franklin. Twenty years later, Noah Webster in his famous spelling book still indicated the [æ] pronunciation for *aunt, jaunt,* and *sauce.*

Nevertheless, soon after 1800 the [ɑ] vowel slowly established itself in British English, at least in that variety spoken in the vicinity of London. There is some evidence pointing to the ironical circumstance that it originated in Cockney speech—ironical because in America the "broad" pronunciation is frequently interpreted as an indication of refinement, especially by the socially and culturally insecure. Walker, for example, in his pronouncing dictionary of 1790 characterized this pronunciation of the vowel as vulgar, and the so-called flat *a* as "characteristic of the elegant and learned world." At all events, despite a wide diversity of usage in London itself, the [ɑ] sound must have gained a firm foothold in southeastern England by the second quarter of the nineteenth century. The question of its extension to coastal New England will be discussed later. The important thing to be noticed here is that American English has retained the older or earlier pronunciation feature, whereas British English, in accepted or Received Standard form, has undergone a more recent development. It is interesting, incidentally, that the older view of Black English as being an extensive collection of archaisms will not fit these facts; the Black pronunciation of *aunty* matches a "recent" British phonological development.

In this connection it should also be realized that the total number of words pronounced with the vowel of *cat* in American English but with that of *father* in British English is relatively small. There are possibly not more than 150 altogether that are in common use, as compared with at least three times as many which regularly have the [æ] sound in both American and British English. Conversely, the historical "short *a*" has regularly become [ɑ]

before *r* and in a few other isolated words in both Britain
and America. For the most part the words which vary between the
"flat" and the "broad" *a* are those in which the vowel is followed
by a voiceless fricative (*f, s,* or *th,* as in *thin*) or by *n.*

The same general conclusion holds for the differences between
Received Standard British and general American practice in such
words as *firm, earth, turn,* and *word.* Originally these had the
vowel indicated by their present spelling followed by consonantal
r. Thus *firm* would have had the vowel of *bit, earth* the vowel of
get, turn the vowel of *good,* and *word* the vowel of *fork.* There is
some reason for believing that by Shakespeare's time the various
vowels had begun to coalesce with the following *r* to produce a
vowel something like our present-day sound of *err;* in fact, there is
evidence for its existence in London lower- or lower-middle-class
dialect as early as 1560. Presumably, as time went on, the vowel
of *err* came to be pronounced in southern England with less and
less of the *r*-coloring, until by the close of the eighteenth century
the consonantal *r* had been lost completely. The same development took place with *r* before consonants, as in *ford,* and after
vowels in word-final position, as in *far.*

We learn, for example, from Walker's *Rhyming Dictionary* of
1775 that *aunt* and *haunch* were pronounced "nearly as if written
arnt and *harnch.*" This does not mean that an *r* was inserted in
aunt but rather than the r of *aren't* was scarcely audible at this
time. And in his *Pronouncing Dictionary* of 1791, the same lexicographer tells us that, "in England, and particularly in London,
the *r* in *bar, bard, card, regard,* etc., is pronounced so much in the
throat as to be little more than the middle or Italian *a,* lengthened
into *baa, baad, caad, regaad.*" He adds that in London, "It is
sometimes entirely sunk."

Whether these statements are interpreted to mean that at this
time British English had merely a weakened *r* or had lost the
sound altogether does not matter greatly. The point is that the English *r*'s were losing their retroflex quality, one which has been retained in the speech of the vast majority of Americans. Here, as

with the "flat" *a,* American English has preserved a feature of the language which was subsequently altered in British English.

A few other less obvious differences between the stressed vowels of American and British English point to the same general conclusion. The vowel of British English *sun* and *cut* is more open than the corresponding American sound; it is made with the jaw in a slightly lower position and possibly with the tongue somewhat more advanced, giving it a timbre more like that of the sound of [ɑ]. During the last 500 years this sound has developed from one which was undoubtedly like our present stressed vowel in the word *good,* made with the jaw in fairly close or high position and with the tongue concentrated or bunched in the back of the mouth. It is fairly evident, therefore, that in British English the sound has undergone the more radical modification and that American English undoubtedly preserves an intermediate stage in its development.

Likewise, the marked tendency in American English, or at least in some areas of the United States, to pronounce the so-called "short *o*" with an [ɑ]-like quality in words like *got, crop, hot, God, stock,* and *frog,* appears to have had its origin in a fashionable pronunciation of the seventeenth century. The difference between British and American pronunciation here is chiefly one of lip-rounding, the vowels being pronounced with spread lips in American English and with slightly pursed or rounded lips in England. The comedies of the Restoration period abound in spellings suggesting unrounded pronunciations of the vowels in these words, both by the fops and the true-wit characters. Moreover, there were in the seventeenth and eighteenth centuries a number of books on English pronunciation written for foreigners who wanted to learn English. In these, English short *o* is very often equated with French or German *a,* also suggesting a pronunciation with spread instead of rounded lips. Again, American English seems to preserve a feature of the language characteristic of British English pronunciation 200 or 300 years ago, although in this par-

ticular instance British pronunciation could be considered as pre-
serving an even older variety of the sound.

In the matter of unstressed syllables, the chief difference in the
pronunciation of the two countries is to be found in the greater retention of secondary stress in American English. British English
tends to collapse the third syllable of words like *secretary, necessary, millinery, oratory,* and at times to reduce the secondary
stress of such other plurisyllables as *circumstance* or *corrobo-
rative.* The presence of secondary stress in the *-ary, -ery, -ory*
words in the pronunciation of Shakespeare is indicated by the
prosody of Hamlet's famous line, "Customary suits of solemn
black." Christopher Cooper in *The English Teacher* (1687) and
Elphinston in *The Principles of the English Language,* as late as
1765, still indicated the presence of secondary stress in these
words. Here too the elimination of the secondary stress appears to
have been a late-eighteenth- and early-nineteenth-century development in England not shared by speakers of American English.

It seems also that the pronunciation of the final syllables of
words like *fertile* and *hostile* with the sound of *file* is a fairly
recent British development. Earlier authorities on pronunciation
generally indicate the vowel of *fill* for the second syllable of these
words—the general practice in the United States today. Turning to
the consonants, we may observe that the initial *wh* combination in
such words as *whale* and *wharf* is quite regularly simplified to *w*
in southern British English, but in the United States there is a
much stronger tendency to retain the earlier pronunciation.

British-American differences in the pronunciation of individual
words rather than those representing a whole class of sounds
usually show the present British pronunciation to be the more
recent development. This is true, for example, of *hover,* regularly
pronounced in America with the vowel of *cut,* but often in England with the vowel of *hot.* The derivation of this word is uncer-
tain, but early spellings leave little doubt that the present American pronunciation is the traditional one. Similarly, the American

pronunciation of *schedule,* with *sk* rather than *sh,* appears to have been an earlier British pronunciation. The one now prevailing in England was probably generally adopted during the second quarter of the nineteenth century.

The spelling bee, a prominent factor in American colonial and frontier life, is sometimes advanced as a possible explanation of certain phonetic features of American English. It is argued that the practice of spelling and pronouncing words a syllable at a time could have been responsible for the retention of strong secondary stress as well as the maintenance of the "retroflex" quality in our *r* sounds. Both of these theories are questionable. The spelling bee in itself could hardly have had such widespread influence. If we consider it, however, as another manifestation of an awareness of formal style and literary tradition available to the frontiersman only through books, we may be on the trail of something significant. It must also be remembered that American and British English differ, in a factor such as the assignment of stress, in only a small minority of the plurisyllables in the vocabulary.

The preponderance of immigrant stocks learning English in the New World has also been advanced as an explanation of these American tendencies. It has been assumed that first- and second-generation speakers of English were more likely to pronounce words just as they were spelled. It is, however, difficult to see why such "foreign" pronunciations would recapitulate the particular pronunciation features of older English.

In certain of its superficial grammatical aspects, American English has some resemblance to earlier stages of the language. There are, it is true, relatively few inflectional differences in the standard forms of British and American, but one of the most prominent will illustrate the principle. British English has but one past participle for the verb *get,* namely the form *got.* American English has, in addition, the form *gotten,* which no speaker of British English uses regularly, and which many Britons assume to be the only American form. Consequently, English novelists frequently portray

American characters using *gotten* in situations where the word would never occur in normal American speech.

In fact, most Americans regularly make a very precise distinction between *got* and *gotten*. "We've *got* ten thousand dollars for laboratory equipment," means that the funds in question are in our possession—we now have them. "We have *gotten* ten thousand dollars for laboratory equipment," means that we have obtained or acquired this particular sum of money although it may not yet be in our possession. Few Americans would have the slightest question about the difference in the meaning of these two sentences.

Get is a so-called strong (or "irregular") verb which, in the process of normal development, would have had a form like *gat* for the past tense (which is actually the case in the Authorized Version of the Bible) and *getten* as its past participle. Somehow or other the verb was reworked or re-formed according to the pattern of such verbs as *bear* and *tear;* it developed *got* as its past-tense form and *got* or *gotten* as its past participle. In England *gotten* seems not to have continued in use beyond the mid- or late-seventeenth century, but Americans have continued to employ it up to the present time. So much for the purely morphological aspect of the construction; there is a syntactical element to be considered as well.

After the verb *have* came to be more widely used as an auxiliary, it tended to lose force as an indicator of possession. Consequently the verb *get* in its perfect tense form tended, during the sixteenth century, to shift its meaning from acquisition to that of possession, much as Spanish *tener* replaced *haber* as the latter became an auxiliary. Shakespeare, Swift, Johnson, Thackeray, and Ruskin are all attested as using *have got* for the possessive. This seems to have spread to America soon after its development, although even today some Americans mistakenly feel that that the construction is somewhat less elegant or less correct than the simple verb *have*, and virtually no American naturally uses *had got* as the equivalent of *had*. "He had not got a shilling for the meter," becomes "He didn't have . . ." in American English. The continued existence of the older *gotten* made possible the distinction between *have gotten* and *have got* in America, which the English, confined to the single form *got*, could not develop in precisely the same manner. "We got something" is an informal reduction from *have got* in the speech of most Americans—*have* will reappear if the statement is negated, although it may take the form of *ain't* in some casual styles. In Black English, however, *we got something* is negated as *we don't got* . . . —showing that *have* has not been a functional part of the expression's derivational history.

Another structural difference between American and British English is to be found in the much stronger tendency in the latter toward the use of plural verbs and plural pronouns of reference with collective nouns. Words like *government, ministry, cabinet, company, corporation,* and names of athletic teams regularly govern the plural rather than the singular number. A sentence such as, The government *are* acting like *themselves,"* quoted from Robert Southey by the *Oxford English Dictionary,* is characteristically British and quite impossible for an American.

No one seems to have studied the development of the plural with these collectives. Originally the singular would have been demanded, but as early as 1000, plural verbs began to appear with collective nouns when the idea of a number of individuals took precedence over the group concept. This is the way collectives were used in Shakespeare's time, and it is the way they are still used in the United States. The consistent use of the plural with certain of these nouns apparently developed in England in the second quarter of the nineteenth century. Southey is the *Oxford English Dictionary* source for plural agreement with *corporation* as well as *government. Ministry* appears in this construction somewhat later. American English has retained the older practice, and as yet no indications of a change have appeared.

The tendency of American English to retain features of the earlier language needs no further elaboration. We have found evidence of it in the vocabulary, in pronunciation, in inflectional forms, and in syntax. Nor is English the only language in which a colonial offshoot shows a tendency toward archaism. Canadian French reflects features of continental French antedating the revolution. Older elements of European Spanish may be seen in the current idiom of any number of Latin American countries, and it is well known that modern Icelandic has been less affected by linguistic change than Norwegian of the present day.

Moreover, if we turn to certain other aspects of our natural life, we find that America has kept alive a number of elements of its cultural heritage which are quite absent, or at best much less conspicuous, in the England of today than at the time they were brought to this country.

The religious or theological background of the colonies provides an excellent case in point. During the early settlement of New England, the Calvinism of Oliver Cromwell and his followers was the dominating force in the mother country. It has been characterized by Max Savelle in *The Foundations of American Civilization* (1942) as, "The major item in the religious inheritance of the Americans from Great Britain." The Puritanism of New England was later reinforced by the Calvinism of the Dutch and the Scotch-Irish, both of whom came in considerable numbers and were influential in our subsequent development. "Today," says Russell Blankenship, "Puritanism as a religious faith has quite largely disappeared from New England as it has from other parts of the country, but it exists all over the nation as a moral force, an influence constantly directing our attention to the fact that life is a most serious business and that everything must be judged in terms of current morality." In this respect, Puritanism is still a strong force in American life and thought.

The blood feud, which provides the motivation for many of the ballads, chronicles, and other literature of Scotland and the border counties, appears in a sense to have been reactivated in the Kentucky and West Virginia mountains during the third quarter of the last century. The violent hatreds and gory exploits of the Hatfields

and the McCoys have virtually become folk legend in the United
States, and certain aspects of the saga (such as its origin in a quar-
rel over the ownership of a pig) have a quaintly humorous flavor.
This particular altercation was merely the most notorious of a
fairly large number. Both the racial stock of the participants and
the settlement history of the entire mountain area leave little question that Kentucky feuding was, in essence, a transference and
prolongation of the same culture trait from the Scottish border
country.

A less dramatic but even more characteristic transference is
found in American patchwork quilt patterns, many of which preserve figures and designs which were brought over from England.
Miss Elizabeth King, in her pamphlet *Quilting,* commented that
the "feather" quilting pattern found on many early American
quilts was the one that had been used in Northumberland since
1600. Without question other patterns would, upon investigation,
reveal a similar history. Homemade quilts, to continue that example, have been regularly exhibited at our county fairs, but British officials have found some difficulty in finding quilts for their
expositions. This culture trait has obviously been kept alive in the
United States while disappearing in England.

A final and well-known illustration of the preservation of old-
country ways is offered by the folk ballads. At least fifty-five separate airs were transported and preserved. The well-known *Barbara
Allen,* for example, existed, according to a mid-twentieth-century
study, in the largest numbers of both tunes and texts.

While these linguistic and cultural archaisms are being detailed,
it is well to keep in mind that the same observers who saw archaism in early America were also struck by the unprecedented innovations. If Anglo-Saxon folksongs preserve older English traditions, Black folk music does so only with the most extreme kind of
modification. A familiar example is "The Darby Ram," in some
sense the source for the New Orleans jazz number played on the
way back from the graveyard, "Didn't He Ramble?" Comparison
of texts, not to mention music, shows some early English influ-

ence, it is true, but even more adaptation to Afro-American patterns. The Anglo-Saxon archaic survivals did influence the other ethnic groups, but the influences are often intermixed to the point of genuine syncretism.

Much research effort has been expended in identifying American retentions from earlier times, but the positively identified features are far from overwhelming either in number or in distribution. One inescapable conclusion is that although colonial lag must have been a factor in the development of American English, it is rather trivial when compared to features like that of the contact with other languages and cultures.

Although not studied as much, the elimination of differences between different dialects known as leveling must also have been an important factor in the development of American culture. While the old ballads are represented in our folk music, it is impossible to say that the ballads of one region of England came to only one region of the United States. Neither has any appreciable body of English regional dialect forms been found in any one specific American dialect. The mobility, social and geographic, which characterized us from the first and throughout all stages of our history has just about eliminated that possibility.

The media in the last few years have given us another, special kind of mobility. In the areas of crafts and other cultural functions, this has been a cause of regret to many people. The oft-mentioned fact that local food terms are giving way to the national terms promulgated commercially and by advertising campaigns is but one example of what has been going on for a long time. Newspaper advertising was an important feature of American life during the late-eighteenth century. Future research is not likely to uncover any hitherto unknown body of archaic language or customs. The case for colonial lag must rest with what has now been familiar for several decades.

The combination of archaism and leveling observable in the British immigrant sector of the American population in the first three-quarters of the eighteenth century could not last in the face of the dynamism of institutions, peoples, and technological developments. Great changes took place in the following century. To some extent, those changes can be explained in terms of contact with languages and cultures, but there are many other changes—and even directions of change—which cannot precisely be linked to any such external influence. Innovation, internally motivated so far as anyone can now tell, seems to have been the strongest ongoing force implementing change.

5
Innovation, Compounding, Derivation, and Tall Talk

Although borrowings from other languages can be rather neatly categorized, and even archaic survivals can be handled in a manner with which almost everyone will agree, differences of opinions and controversy still remain. It is obvious that many such changes did take place. Since neither archaic retentions nor the incorporation of non-English elements explain all that is characteristic of the English language in America, the language historian must also concern himself with the innovations that have developed on this side of the Atlantic. These are evident chiefly in the vocabulary, although the factor of derivation, which has both grammatical and syntactic consequences, enters into the picture as well.

To offer reasons for these changes is to risk a great deal of imprecision, despite the fact that there have been many "explanations." One of those most frequently offered has been the very freedom of the frontier, and the escape from conventional restraints in other matters, including morals, which encouraged an analogous liberty in language. It is true that the frontier has been an extremely important element in our national life. Many historians have followed the lead of Frederick Jackson Turner in find-

ing that the "really American part of our history" must be traced
to the men who grew up under frontier conditions. The belief—
myth, if it is that—has been so strong that John Kennedy, one of
the most popular presidents of the twentieth century, made his national appeal in terms of developing a "New Frontier." Yet we
can draw no conclusions about the development of American English without considering a large amount of data and many specific instances.

A development in the field of grammar will serve as the first
topic for investigation. This is the phenomenon that is sometimes
called functional change, a feature of many languages but an especially prominent one in contact languages. In most languages
various parts of speech have what might be called characteristic
shapes. Thus, in Spanish so many nouns end in -o and -a that
these endings come to be felt as definite marks of the substantive.
Verb infinitives generally end in -ar, -er, and -ir, and these termi-
nations in their turn are associated with the verbal function. It is
possible for a Spanish noun to be made into a verb, or even for the
reverse process to take place, but the transition does involve an alteration of what has been called the characteristic shape of the
word, and consequently such changes are not too common.

English, on the other hand, has lost its inflections to such a
degree that transitions from noun to adjective, from verb to noun
(to ride to a ride), from adjective to verb (from warm milk to to
warm the milk), and in fact, in almost all conceivable directions,
are made constantly. They are so thoroughly an ingrained part of
the language that a word such as down may actually perform five
different part-of-speech functions: preposition, adverb, adjective
(down on someone), noun (a down in football), and verb.

Occasionally such derivation falls into disfavor with teachers
and rhetoricians. This has happened to contact used as a verb,
which is frowned upon as commercial or possibly journalistic
jargon by many people today. However, where one word will
acquire a temporary taboo, a dozen others will shift their functions without attracting unfavorable notice. In a good many in-

stances functional changes of this nature have occurred in American English but not in British, or some time has elapsed before the word appeared in its changed function in England. At least coincidentally, the American frontier was the locus of pidgin varieties (Black, Indian, and Chinese) in which such functional changes were much more prevalent than in ordinary varieties of English. These special contact varieties have, also, consistently been held in low regard by educators and rhetoricians.

Undoubtedly the most frequent kind of derivational change which is encountered is that of noun to adjective, or perhaps it would be more accurate to say the use of nouns in an adjunct or joined function. For example, almost as soon as the noun *caucus* had been borrowed from the Indian language, it was employed in the combinations *caucus men* (1762) and *caucus clubs* (1763). The tendency to use nouns as modifiers is evidenced particularly in headlines, where such astounding combinations as CLUB FIGHT BLOCKS RIVER RAIL TUBE PLAN (organizational dispute interferes with plans for a rail tunnel under the river) greet the eye from time to time. A verbatim citation taken from the luncheon menu of a metropolitan department store, *Butter Cream Frosted Devil's Food Pecan Layer Cake,* illustrates an extension of the same tendency to some of our food terms.

The shift in the opposite direction, from adjective to noun, is neatly illustrated by the following advertisement from a current newspaper, which is headed BASIC DRESSES, and then goes on to read, "A group of conservatively styled basics to accessorize as you will." An earlier illustration of the same type of change is offered by *personal,* referring to a newspaper item, cited in 1864.

The conversion of nouns to verbs is also very common. *Clapboard* is recorded as a verb as early as 1637, which must have been not long after the colonists began to cut and plane timber into finished building materials. The verbal use of *scalp,* perhaps projected onto the Indians rather than actually part of their practice, occurred early: *tomahawk,* another stereotypical term for assumed Indian methods of warfare, appears as a verb in 1711.

Other aspects of colonial and frontier life are reflected by *portage* (1836), *lynch* (1835), and *deed* (1806). The reluctance toward changes of this nature is well illustrated in connection with the last word. It was included in John Pickering's *Vocabulary or Collection of Words and Phrases Which Have Been Supposed to be Peculiar to the United States of America,* which, appearing in 1816, was one of the earliest lists of Americanisms. Pickering's comment with reference to the verb *deed* is, "We sometimes hear this word used colloquially; but rarely except by illiterate people."

On occasion the conversion of noun into verb had to await the development of a special American meaning. This was true with *lumber.* In England, the noun *lumber* meant cumbersome, useless material, apparently having been formed from the verb *to lumber.* In America, however, very early in the colonial period, the noun *lumber* was applied to cut timber. Finally, in the nineteenth century, *to lumber* came to be used both transitively and intransitively, meaning to be in the lumber business or to cut the timber off a piece of land. Likewise, *to stag it*—that is, for a man to attend a mixed party alone—could only have developed from the noun *stag,* "a man not escorting a lady," which in turn grew out of such combinations as *stag dance, stag dinner, stag party*—all peculiar to America. *Interview* as a verb is an American development of the special journalistic use of the noun; both are first cited in 1869. For at least the first two decades of their existence both verb and noun were quite regularly enclosed in quotation marks, and in England were used only in a somewhat jocular sense.

Nor has the process diminished with the years. Though not exclusively American, the noun *thumbtack* is commonly used in the United States for what is more frequently called a *drawing pin* in England, but the verb *to thumbtack* has thus far been cited only from American sources, from 1931 on. Likewise in this country *automobile* as a verb (1898) followed hard upon the heels of the application of the term to the self-propelled vehicle in 1895.

Unless we attribute this process to the contact languages encountered in the New World, the only explanation seems to be that most of the accretions to the American vocabulary from other languages were nouns; so too are many of the compound and derivative formations. Once a thing is named, we are likely to require as well a term for its operative or verbal aspect, and functional change provides an easy solution to the problem.

The development of nouns from verbs is somewhat less common, although instances are by no means lacking. The noun *dump* as a place for waste and refuse was formed from the verb as early as 1784. The verb *sashay,* borrowed from French in 1836, was converted into a noun in 1900. As we have seen, Henry David Thoreau is credited with the first American citation of the English dialect verb *drool* in 1854; the earliest citation for *drool* as a substantive is 1867. The verb *scoop* in its journalistic sense developed as a specialization of the slang meaning, "to get the advantage of," which later gave rise to the noun *scoop* for a so-called newspaper "beat," and in fact this use of the noun *beat* came about in precisely the same way. Similarly, *release* as a noun indicating a news story given out for publication is first recorded in 1907, only three years after the earliest citation of the verb in this special journalistic sense. *Strike* used as a noun, both in baseball and in American bowling, has clearly developed from the verb; so has *cut,* meaning a reduction in prices or wages.

Drive used substantively in connection with cattle, logs, an organized campaign for collecting funds, or in the more general sense of initiative or impulse, is a striking illustration of the development of a noun from a verb in the United States. *Probe,* meaning an investigation, appears to have been as great a favorite with headline writers at the beginning of the century as it is today. *Pick-up,* for a light delivery truck, is a recent (1944) instance of the same tendency.

Other types of functional change include developments of verb to modifier as in *take-out food,* or even *brown and serve rolls.* The change from adjective to verb can be illustrated by *to prep,* from *prep,* the clipped adjective form of *preparatory school.*

In addition to its frequent alteration of word function, American English often has a peculiar manner of putting words and word elements together. Basically, of course, all the Teutonic languages are much given to compounding, although the tendency is possibly most noticeable in German because of its characteristic fashion of writing compounds as single words. Often the English equivalent for a German term happens not to be parallel in function, as in *Feldmesskunst,* "the science of surveying." Even if the terms correspond exactly in the two languages, as in *Fire Insurance Company* compared with *Feuerversicherungsgesellschaft,* the German word by virtue of its length and solidity impresses one with its compound construction, whereas the corresponding fact in English may totally escape the writer or speaker.

Still, we do have a great deal of compounding in English; it is a heritage of the oldest period of the language, when such felicitous constructions as *whale road* for "ocean," *hammer leaving* for "sword," and *peace weaver* for "queen," known as kennings, constituted one of the characteristic rhetorical devices of our earliest poetry. But the device survived the purely Teutonic period of our language. A page of Shakespeare yields "something-settled," "periwig-pated," "queen mother," "town crier," and "to out-Herod." It has been pointed out, moveover, that although many centuries ago English replaced its original *book house* with the French borrowing *library,* the language has subsequently coined such combinations as *bookshop, bookbinder, bookcase, book collector, book fair, booklover, book review, bookroom, book sale,* and *book trade.* These are only a few of the 115 combinations recorded by the *Oxford English Dictionary,* to which may be added *book agent, book bindery, book count, book factor, book farmer, book farming, book concern, book peddler,* and *book social.* All of these are American in origin, as is the more recent *book club.*

American English in particular has demonstrated a fondness for compound formations, one which not only goes back to its earliest beginnings but which frequently seems to have the earmarks of an indigenous style. In the records of the Lewis and Clark expedition, for example, 171 previously unrecorded Americanisms, consisting of general terms, contain 106 full-word combinations. Of 412 previously unrecorded American names for plants and animals, 129 are compounds. Of the 301 terms for which these journals supply earlier examples than had been previously recorded, 132 are compound words. Just a few of the combined forms culled from these entries include *arrowwood, bull snake, ground squirrel, tumble bug, cut-off, copperhead, cottonwood, catbird, bottom land,* and *tow-cord.*

The same strong tendency toward the formation of compounds is evident from a study of the individual word-entries in the *Dictionary of Americanisms.* There are twenty compound words with *stage* as a first element, forty-seven formed from *beaver,* and over one hundred with *yellow* or with a combination already formed from the word (*yellow-dog contract*).

The whole question of compounding in American English can best be discussed in terms of the particular domains of the vocabulary in which the process has taken place. Moreover, the creation of compounds upon a large scale in these areas seems to have been in response to several distinct classes of situations.

First of all, there were the fields in which physical conditions prevailing in America presented a considerable degree of change from those characteristic of England. For example, many of the flora and fauna in the northern part of the colonies were similar to but not identical with the plant and animal life of England. Where differences did exist, new terminology had to be provided, to which the 129 compounds of the Lewis and Clark accounts bear impressive testimony. Many of our compounds in these fields are very early: *live oak* is found in *A True Declaration of the Estate of the Colonie in Virginia,* 1610. *Bull frog* is first recorded in 1698, *ground hog* in 1656, *swamp oak* in 1681, *coach whip snake* in 1736. Differences in topography are reflected in *bottom land,* 1728; *water gap,* 1756; and *underbrush,* 1775. Even the weather is represented by *cold snap,* 1776.

Institutions were also liable to change in a new environment, and the changes brought a new terminology with them. Farming, carried on under totally different conditions, both physical and economic, developed such combinations as *log house, log cabin, corn belt, cotton gin, round up, land office, hog ranch, stump fence, worm fence, hired man, hired girl, hired hand,* and *hired help.* American independence brought in its wake the development of institutions and practices peculiar to this country. So extensive was the political and governmental terminology which resulted that a whole volume has been written about it: witness *lame duck, boss rule, favorite son, dark horse, carpetbagger,* and *peanut politics* (long before Jimmy Carter!) as a random sampling of our North American formations.

When we consider peculiarly American developments, the proportion of compounds in the terminology becomes even greater. Baseball, in its present form a distinctively American game, applies compound terms to every specific position on the team except for the catcher and the pitcher. The four bases, the home plate, the infield, the outfield, chest protectors, and various types of gloves are all compounds. There have developed, moreover, any number of compound terms associated with the game: *pinch-hit, bush league, double-header, grandstand play, college try, charley horse,* and *rain check.* Basketball, a fairly recent American innovation, is just as full of compounds: the almost obsolete *center jump* and the more current *power forward, playmaker, slam dunk,* etc. The somewhat more sedentary game of poker has *full house, straight flush, jackpot, penny ante,* and *seven-card stud,* among many others.

The first *soda fountain* seems to have originated in Boston in 1824. Ever since that time the array of ice-cream sodas, the sundaes, the banana splits, the varieties of milk shakes, malted and otherwise, has resulted in a terminology consisting almost entirely of compounds. Even *Coca-Cola,* the insidious fifth-column of American culture, described in 1887 as a "brain tonic and intellectual soda-fountain beverage," has the appearance of a combined form.

A third type of situation arose when a new invention or development struck America and England at the same time, resulting in the creation of terminologies quite independent of each other. The railroad offers an early instance of this; the automobile, radio, and now television are later examples. For example, in American railroad terms there are such combinations as *boxcar, handcar, chair car, jerkwater, waybill, stopover, sideswipe, milk train, hog engine, sidetrack,* and *roundhouse.* When rail travel gave way almost exclusively to the automobile in the 1960's, some of the terms remained in American usage although they were perhaps not always understood in the old way: a "jerkwater" town remained a small town, although not everyone who used the term realized that it referred to a locomotive taking on water. If the gasoline shortage of the 1980's brings back the passenger train as an important factor in transportation, it will be interesting to see whether the old terminology revives or a new one is born.

In conclusion we must ask whether any special qualities are discernible in the American compounds. Certainly one receives, from a listing of any number of them, the impression of a somewhat peculiar flavor. Even such a small group as *sweatshop, disc jockey, speakeasy, rat race, soap opera, zoot suit,* and *wetback* seems to have something indigenous about it when compared with British *goods van, wood wool, drop-head coupé, motor car hire service,* and *screw spanner.*

Frequently the American compound is elliptical rather than self-explanatory. *Soap opera* is not immediately clear to the uninitiated (any more than is *horse opera*). One needs to know that romances of the boy-meets-girl type or accounts of supposedly typical American family life, presented in seemingly never-ending installments on American television, are frequently sponsored by manufacturers of toilet and laundry soaps, and are directed to the housewife who goes about her daily tasks with her set turned on. For a comprehension of *wetback,* it must be realized that annually large numbers of Mexican laborers enter the United States by the simple expedient of swimming or wading across the Rio Grande, thereby avoiding quota restrictions and immigration formalities. Hence the physically descriptive appellative. *Car hop, straw hat theater,* and *strip tease* likewise require a cultural footnote for the foreigner.

Metaphor plays a considerable part in these American combinations. A *disc jockey* has nothing to do with horses; he is an employee of a radio station and conducts a program of recorded music. *Rat race, captive mine, ghost town, double talk,* all employ one of their elements figuratively. Finally there is often a strong element of incongruity in the two or more parts comprising the combination: note *taxi-dancer, prowl car, squawk box, prairie schooner, cow college,* and *nose cone.*

New words may also be formed, not by combining full or independent words but by the addition of prefixes or suffixes to a single word. Here, too, American English has found a fertile field for its inventiveness. The *Dictionary of Americanisms* lists no less than 105 combinations with the prefix *anti-,* for example. These range all the way from *anti-federalist,* through *anti-secession* and *anti-Mormon,* up to *anti-braintruster* and *anti-C.I.O.* Other prefixes which have been particularly fruitful are *de-, pro-, semi-,* and *super-,* the last of these bearing witness to the national tendency toward hyperbole—particularly in the area of sports, where terms like *Superbowl, superstar,* and *Super Dome* abound.

Some of the suffixes which have been employed to a considerable extent in American English include *-ette,* which serves the function of a feminine marker in *usherette, drum-majorette,* and *Rockette* (a dancer in the chorus line of the Radio City Music Hall in New York's Rockefeller Center), and that of a diminutive in *kitchenette, dinette,* and *bathinette.* The suffix *-ee,* usually indicating a verbal object, appears as early as 1870 in *contestee,* this time with subjective force, and also later in *escapee.* Actually, one might almost trace an American soldier's progress through World War II in terms of this suffix beginning with *draftee* or *selectee,* proceeding to *rejectee, inductee,* and *trainee,* going on to the seat of the conflict with *liberee* and *evacuee*, and concluding his career as a *separatee*.

Place designation is indicated by *-ite* in *Camdenite, New Jerseyite;* but the suffix has a broader classificatory function in *socialite, laborite, trailerite,* and the punning *third-termite,* coined during Franklin D. Roosevelt's presidential campaign of 1940.

Both *-ster* and *-eer* seem to have acquired unfavorable connotations in *gangster, speedster, racketeer, sloganeer,* and *black marketeer.* The suffix *-itis* is playfully pejorative in *golfitis, conventionitis, radioitis,* and *headlinitis,* but it is worth noting that *appendicitis* is also of American origin. The desire to give a professional aura to occupations deserving of somewhat less has led to formations in *-ist, -ician,* and *-tor: receptionist, cosmetist, cosmetician, beautician, mortician,* and *realtor.*

Most of the combinations mentioned so far have been nouns. The suffix *-ize* has been frequently employed to create new verbs: *itemize, accessorize, demoralize, burglarize, slenderize, simonize, winterize, hospitalize,* as well as *Americanize,* and *Sanforize.* In this connection it is interesting to observe that as early as 1591, in his introduction to Sir Philip Sidney's *Astrophel and Stella,* Thomas Nashe castigated the "reprehenders that complain of my boisterous compound words and ending my Italianate coined words all in *ize.*" This suggests, perhaps, that the creative exuberance generated by the frontier culture in America paralleled a similar impetus in the Elizabethan language.

The suffix *-er* is undoubtedly one of the earliest to have been used to form peculiarly American coinages. A citation for 1654–5 indicates that a *corder* was a town official whose function it was to pile salable wood into standard cords. More modern behavior patterns give us *teenybopper* and *rock and roller* from music, *women's libber* and *bra-burner* from the feminist movement, *gas guzzler* to replace obsolete *hay burner* in transportation, and *doper* and *tripper* from the drug culture.

One interesting difference between British and American English is to be found in the use of the *-ery* suffix, which in England is often used for a class of materials (*drapery*) or the place where an occupation or operation is carried on (*colliery*) but seldom for the establishment where the product is sold at retail. Thus, *bakery* in England refers to the craft of the baker or the place for making bread, rather than to the place where baked goods are available to the consumer, as the term has been used in the United States since 1827. Likewise, *grocery,* used in England for the merchandise itself since the fifteenth century, was applied to a retail establishment in America as early as 1659.

Conversely, American English uses *cook* in combinations such as *cookbook, cook stove,* where British English has *cookery;* and such familiar English terms as *ironmongery, deanery, farmery,* and *rockery* sound strange to an American ear. Moreover, some of the *-ery* combinations which do not indicate a retail establishment, though originally formed in this country, have had a short life here. *Printery* was used as early as 1638 in Massachusetts, but has now been replaced by *print shop* or when it applies to an official bureau by *printing office. Loggery* for a log cabin, first used in Michigan in 1839, lasted less than half a century.

Another process or device common in English is that of shortening words by clipping—the omission of syllables from the beginning or end. This had gone to such lengths in the seventeenth and early eighteenth centuries that Addison objected to it in a frequently quoted statement from one of the *Spectator* papers that specified *"mob, rep, pos, incog,* and the like." But he concluded, "I dare not answer for these that they will not in time be looked upon as a part of our tongue."

Despite this protest, which was echoed if not anticipated by Jonathan Swift in one of the *Tatler* essays and in his *Proposal for Correcting the English Tongue,* the tendency to clip words has continued on both sides of the Atlantic. The English have contributed *photo, spats, van,* and *wig* to the language, to mention only a few. The erroneous notion that this shortening process was indigenous to the United States was set forth at the turn of the century by the *Boston Herald,* which declared in its issue of July 4, 1899, "If we must Americanize and shorten the word, why not call them 'autos'?" The point is that the Americans and the British have not always clipped the same words.

Nevertheless, the mistaken notion of the Boston newspaper is understandable, for in noting the dates of the earliest appearances of some of our commonest words in this category, one comes to realize how common the practice was just at that time. *Co-ed* put in its first appearance in 1889, *gym* in 1897, *gas* for "gasoline" in 1905, and *movie* in 1906. This last item suggests also the short-lived *talkie,* first appearing in 1913. More recent was *prefab,* 1942. Even more recently we have *narc* (narcotics agent), *mono* (monophonic), and *stereo* (stereophonic). These are all shortenings which have retained the initial part of the word and have elimi-nated the final portion.

The reverse process is seen in *sang* for "ginseng," 1843; *stogie* for "Conestoga" (boot or cigar), 1847; *pike* for "turnpike" in 1852—the application of this to the road itself rather than to the toll is particularly American—*phone* in 1886, *coon* for "raccoon," and *pop* for "soda pop." We tend to handle a lot of our place names in a similar way: Las Vegas is *Vegas* and San Francisco, *Frisco,* to many who consider themselves sophisticated in the ways of American cities. Foreign names are also affected: Viet Nam be-came *Nam* to many who fought there. The process goes on contin-uously, but the rate at which the words are adopted into the stan-dard language varies a great deal.

A special analogical type of the shortening process has come to be known as back formation. It operates as follows: There are in English a large number of verbs ending in *-ate* which have corre-sponding derivative noun forms in *-ation.* Thus we have *create, creation; deviate, deviation; bifurcate, bifurcation; placate, placa-tion; ruminate, rumination.* This gives rise to a pattern of verb in *-ate* alongside the noun in *-ation.* The English language, however, borrowed a few nouns in *-ation* for which the corresponding verb in *-ate* did not originally exist. When, from a noun of this type, the corresponding verb in *-ate* is then created, the process is called back formation.

It was in this fashion that the verb *donate* was formed from the noun *donation*. It first appeared in America in 1795, almost a century before any British writer ventured to use it. As late as 1935 Herbert Horwill called it "a word which in England is eschewed by good writers as a pretentious and magniloquent vulgarism. In America on the other hand, it has acquired a place in the vocabulary of quite respectable terms." Earlier, however, it had the dubious distinction of a place in William Cullen Bryant's famous *Index Expurgatorius* and was denounced by Richard Grant White. Today it is firmly established in the United States.

Undoubtedly the earliest of all known American back formations is *locate,* which appeared in a Virginia travel account in 1652. The noun *location* had been taken over into English more than a half-century earlier. Among the early users of *locate* were Benjamin Franklin and George Washington; it acquired respectability in a shorter time and with less of a struggle than some later formations of precisely the same character. *Commute* in the sense of regular railroad travel from a suburban residence into the city developed in a similar manner from *commutation* (ticket, train, etc.) in 1865.

Verbal nouns with other variations of the final *-tion* suffix have given us *locomote,* once slang but now obsolete, *electrocute* in 1889, *emote,* labeled jocose by Webster in 1934, and *injunct,* excoriated by Schele de Vere (a collector of Americanisms) in 1871 as "a violent contraction." He was equally displeased with *excurt* from *excursion,* though he failed to mention *excur,* formed twenty years earlier from the same noun.

From agentive nouns ending in *-er,* we have acquired *to housekeep,* 1842, and *to burgle,* 1870, almost a decade before *The Pirates of Penzance* where Gilbert immortalized the word in the chorus of the policemen, "When the enterprising burglar's not a-burgling." *To baby-sit* was brought to life by the shortage of domestic help in the United States, forcing mothers to depend upon *baby sitters* to care for their children. It is equally natural for *student teachers* to engage in the practice of *student teaching* or *to student teach*.

Miscellaneous creations include *enthuse*, probably coined in this country by a Scotsman in 1827, *jell*, 1869, and *reune*, "to attend a reunion," cited as colloquial in 1929. In general, back formations are not numerous; they are confined mainly to two or three types of suffixes. Some arouse violent objections and remain on the periphery of respectability for a considerable period. Others die out after a short time, but on the whole back formations have contributed their measure of utility to the American variety of English.

American ingenuity has found a much more fertile field in the telescoping of words, to produce what are sometimes known as blends. As with the other changes in form which have been discussed in this chapter, the process is employed in England as well, but not with the same words or word elements. The nonsense verse of Lewis Carroll is the most famous text for such blends. In *Through the Looking Glass,* Carroll explained: "Well, 'slithy' means 'lithe' and 'slimy' . . . there are two meanings packed into one word." And a little later in the same work, " 'Mimsy' is 'flimsy' and 'miserable.' "

Several types of word blending may be recognized. First, there are words which combine a single syllable or two syllables of an initial word with a full or complete second term. Among these are such comparatively recent coinages as *giropilot, moto-rustler,* and *stratochamber. Amerindian* is first cited in 1897.

Possibly somewhat more common are combinations of a complete initial word with part of a second. One of the earliest instances of these recalls an interesting bit of American political history. *Gerrymander* was coined in 1812 from the name of the then governor of Massachusetts, Elbridge Gerry, and the word *salamander*. This was in reference to the peculiarly shaped election district in the northeastern part of the state, devised to maintain a majority for the political party then in control. Other instances of this same process include *cablegram* (cable telegram) 1868, *trav-*

elog (travel monologue) 1893, *newscast* (news broadcast) 1937, *Airacuda* (a fighter bomber named for the barracuda) 1937, and more recently *hydramatic, paratrooper, Skycycle,* and *telecast* (television broadcast, partly on the analogy of *newscast*). The word *rock* (music) has very recently combined with other elements to produce forms like *rockathon* (rock marathon) and *rockabilly* (hillbilly or country music influenced by rock and roll).

The initial portion of a first word may be combined with the final part of a second, as in *urinalysis* 1889, *citrange* (citron, orange) 1904, *motel* (motor hotel), *celtuce* (celery, lettuce). Clare Luce's coinage *globaloney* (global baloney), *trainasium* (training gymnasium), *tiglon* (tiger, lion), and *elevon* (elevator, aileron) are further examples of the same combination pattern. Walter Winchell, a gossip columnist and radio commentator of the World War II period, claimed credit for *infanticipating* (anticipating an infant) and a host of other, often extremely contrived, such compounds. The strange economic picture of the 1970's, in which common stocks failed to rise at a rate to compensate for inflation, gave birth to *stagflation* (*stagnation* plus *inflation*).

Initial letters frequently furnish the basis for what are called acronyms, which strictly speaking include the above type. The term is now more frequently applied, however, to examples like those following. Acronyms of this type may be pronounced as a word, as in *radar* (radio detection and ranging), *UNESCO, Socony* (Standard Oil Company of New York), and *NATO. SALT* (Strategic Arms Limitation Treaty) even has a sequel: *SALT II.* Some acronyms indicate the intention, purpose, or immediacy of a program: *NOW* (National Organization of Women), *AIM* (American Indian Movement), and *ACTION* (American Council to Improve Our Neighborhoods). An occasional ironic application argues in the other direction: *CREEP* (Committee to Re-elect President [Nixon]).

If the word so formed does not lend itself easily to pronunciation, as will frequently happen when consonants are grouped together, the letters themselves may be pronounced, as in *DP* (displaced person), *DDT* (dichloro-diphenyl-trichloroethane), and *ACTH*. Such a combination may be concealed by spelling out the pronunciation usually given the letters involved, as was done with the *Seabees* (C.B., construction battalion) and the *Elsies* (L.C., landing craft) of World War II. When *C. B.* cropped up again in the 1970's for *citizen's band radio,* the pronounced letters were not associated with any independent word elements.

Repetition of letters may be indicated by numbers: *Tri-Delt, Triple A, Four C's* (Conference on College Composition and Communication). At times vowels may be arbitrarily inserted in a series of unpronounceable consonants, as in *Huff-Duff,* the pronunciation given by servicemen to the initials *HF DF* (high frequency direction finder).

Blending has been a favorite outlet for the ingenuity of manufacturers and distributors in coining unique terms for their products. Gasoline refining companies have produced *Mobilgas, Mobiloil, Sunoco,* and *Enarco* (National Refining Company). Other types of merchandise give us *Nabisco, Band-Aid, Alka-Seltzer, Webcor, Philco.* Any single issue of a current American newspaper or magazine will supply dozens of examples.

Scientific terms are often so long and cumbersome that abbreviation of some kind must be resorted to, particularly when they are used by the lay public in nontechnical situations or when they are made commercially available. Thus ACE becomes a convenient short reference for adrenal cortex extract, DOCA for desoxycorticosterone acetate, and DNA for deoxyribonucleic acid. One can certainly appreciate the desirability of creating the blend word *cortisone* if he realizes that it is 17-hydroxy, 11-dehydrocorticosterone hormone.

In public and governmental affairs, a succession of situations and events has been favorable to the development of acronyms. First there came the host of alphabetical agencies which were created in the early years of Franklin Roosevelt's administration. Some of these agencies, like NRA and WPA, had a relatively short life; others, such as RFC and TVA, continue to play an important role in the national scene. CETA, OED, and HEW were even more pervasive in the headlines of the 1970's. Our entry into the Second World War gave rise to some acronyms that were almost inherently short-lived; some of us still recall, however, OPA and WPB.

Military organization, both in battle areas and in the staff room, vastly more complex than it had ever been before, furnished coinages of the SHAEF type and those of the COMINCH and CINCPAC varieties. Moreover, every one of the women's organizations auxiliary to the armed forces employed an acronym for ordinary reference; it will be necessary to mention only the WACS and the WAVES, but the tendency extended to the Marines and Coast Guard as well.

The United States also has a host of organizations with titles, necessarily long because of considerations of accuracy, which have been treated in the same way: WHO and UNESCO are among the most familiar. Up to the present, strangely enough, this tendency has been evident primarily upon a national and international level. It will be fortunate if each of the fifty states does not create its own multitude of terms. There have, however, been some steps in that direction: NEH, National Endowment for the Humanities, has split into state agencies like LEH, Louisiana Endowment for the Humanities.

Fraternal lodges provide another area, more or less peculiar to American life, where we find the initials of the somewhat grandiose and often cryptic titles of the organizations in frequent use, but with a slight difference. Such mysterious combinations as BPOE, KC, FOE, LOOM, AOH are familiar to millions of Americans, but except for KC, YMCA, and YWCA, they are rarely spoken. They tend to remain on a written level of language. The letters KKK are convenient, whatever one thinks of the organization, since few can confidently say whether the middle letter stands for *Kux* or *Klux*.

In considering the final category of American word coinages, the creation or invention of high-sounding, mouth-filling words, it is necessary first to catch the spirit behind the process. This entails looking into American folklore and folk characters. Carl Carmer, in the foreword to his collection of such material, makes a very acute observation. He writes:

> The people of almost every nation in the world except the United States have liked to make up stories about "the little people." Even the American Indians tell some beautiful tales about them. But Americans have been so busy doing big jobs that they have never taken time off to let their minds play with the tiny folk who have magic powers. At the end of a hard day's work the American cowboys or miners or lumber-jacks or applepickers have had their fun out of making up stories about men who could do jobs that could just not be done, and in an impossibly short time with one hand tied behind them. The dreams of American workers, naturally enough, have never been delicate, exquisite, or polite—like most fairy stories. They have been big and powerful, and a strong wind is always blowing through them.

Carmer's last clause accounts for the title, *Hurricane's Children,* that he gave to these stories of such American folk characters as Paul Bunyan, Mike Fink, John Henry, Strap Buckner, and Steam-boat Annie. All of these illustrate the typical exaggeration of the frontiersman and his tales. Paul Bunyan could cut down two trees with a single blow of a double-bladed axe, one with the down-, and the other with the up-stroke. Strap Buckner used to knock down bulls with a single blow of an iron pestle. Mike Fink could jump across rivers; John Henry could carry a bale of cotton under each arm and two on his head.

This frontier exaggeration found a verbal outlet in the "tall talk" characteristic not only of folk heroes but of real individuals as well. One writer has painstakingly defined "tall talk" as "a form of utterance ranging in composition from striking concoc-tions of ingeniously contrived epithets expressing disparagement or encomium, to wild hyperbole, fantastic simile and metaphor, and a highly bombastic display of oratory, employed to impress the listener with the physical prowess or general superiority of the speaker." This is an instance, however, where illustration is more effective than definition, no matter how precise. Davy Crockett, for example, describes himself as:

> . . . fresh from the back-woods, half horse, half alligator, a little touched with snapping turtle, can wade the Mississippi, leap the Ohio, ride a streak of lightning, slide down a honey locust and not get scratched. I can whip my weight in wild-cats, hug a bear too close for comfort, and eat any man opposed to Jackson.

The tendency toward high-flown simile is evident in the speech purported to have been delivered by an Arkansas legislator in opposition to a proposal to change the name—actually the pronunciation of the name—of his state:

> Compare the lily of the valley to the gorgeous sunrise; the discordant croak of the bullfrog to the melodious tones of a nightingale; the classic strains of Mozart to the bray of a Mexican mule; the puny arm of a Peruvian prince to the muscles of a Roman gladiator—but never change the name of Arkansas.

In addition to the braggadocio and the highly figurative language there is evident a tendency toward the invention of high-sounding words. The frontiersman, ring-tailed roarer, half horse and half alligator, described himself as *kankarriferous* and *rambunctious,* his lady love as *angeliferous* and *splendiferous.* With consummate ease he could *teetotaciously exfluncticate* his opponent in a *conbobberation,* that is to say a conflict or disturbance, or *ramsquaddle* him *bodaciously,* after which the luckless fellow would *absquatulate.* (Of these, *conbobberation* at least may be based upon a Pidgin English form: *bob, bobbery* as "noise, disturbance"; the term is attested in the American West and in the maritime trade.) He invented such fanciful animals as the *guyascutus* and the *ricaboo racker.* When deceived he was *hornswoggled;* when bewildered, *obfusticated.* Other terms of the same general nature which might be mentioned include *cahoots, catawampus,*

flusticated, jumpsecute, snollygoster, ripsniptious, slantindicular,
and *elegantiferously.*

There are two things to be observed about these mouth-filling
words. Most of them appear in print during the 1830's and
1840's. The majority of them are built upon a very few suffixes:
-acious, -iferous, -ticate, and *-icute* are prominent among them.

This tendency toward the bizarre creation is a significant feature
of American English which can be accounted for in terms of cultural history and linguistic tradition. It is reminiscent of the ornate
diction of the Elizabethans, which is found in many writers of the
period, but which was particularly evident in such a work as Marston's *Scourge of Villainy.* It was Marston whose outlandish vocabulary was satirized in Jonson's *Poetaster.*

In America this employment of the tumid and the turgid in vocabulary is to be seen in Nathaniel Ward's *The Simple Cobbler of
Aggawam* (1647), a work which has scarcely received the careful
study that its vocabulary deserves. For example, in speaking of the
possibility of religious liberty within a single province, he wrote:
"If the whole conclave of Hell can so compromise, exadverse and
diametricall contradictions, as to compolitize such a multimon-
strous manfrey of heteroclytes and quicquidlibets quietly; I trust I
may say with all humble reverence, they can doe more than the
Senate of Heaven."

There can be no question about Ward's learning. Unusual as his
verbal creations were, they had been formed with a clear idea of
the Latin and Greek meanings of their component parts. In England itself, similar stylistic tendencies on the part of such contemporaries of Ward as Burton and Sir Thomas Browne were overcome later in the seventeenth century by the restraining influences
of the prose of Cowley and Dryden. That the verbally ornate continued in favor in America would seem to be indicated by the
reprinting of Ward's work as late as 1713.

One may easily surmise that the admiration of the big word
spread from the seacoast to the frontier—a very important path,
incidentally, for the spread of influences of many kinds—where

new coinages now became a sport of the unlettered, fitting in neatly with the other hyperbolical characteristics of tall talk. The cowboy and the fur trapper—not to mention the river boatman— did not have Ward's knowledge of Latin and Greek, and their version of that kind of talk would not be so readily resolved into meaningful component parts.

There are other factors that must be considered. There is a documentary gap from the 1713 printing of Ward's book to the frontiersmen of the 1830's, and the first examples of recorded "tall talk." It is also unlikely that a literary tradition could so completely determine the direction of an oral style. The frontiersman had to cope daily with many languages, Indian and European, and strange-sounding, half-understood words were an important part of his linguistic experience. Furthermore, groups now known to have been present on the frontier, like Black trappers and cowboys, had elaborate oral traditions of their own. That of the Blacks has been called "fancy talk" and is related to West Indian traditions which have names like "talking sweet."

It may never be possible to trace frontier tall talk to any one source. Most probably, many elements contributed to it. The frontiersman, not being a literary or linguistic historian, simply found it interesting and expedient to talk in that fashion—and did so.

At any rate, the American of today, like his forefather on the frontier, still loves the mouth-filling phrase. An illustration is Maury Maverick's coinage *gobbledygook* adopted throughout the country in the closing years of the 1940's. As a further example, witness the following statement reputedly used by the coach of the United States basketball team entered in the 1948 Olympic Games: "We've got the world on the hip because American boys have the hucklety-buck and spizorinkum."

The development of the second of these terms is worth noting as fairly typical of this type of coinage. It is derived from an impossible combination of Latin *specie,* "money," and *rectum,* "the right kind," and was used apparently in frontier areas during the mid-nineteenth century for "hard" money as opposed to greenbacks or paper currency. It then acquired meanings as diverse as "tireless energy" and "tawdry adornment" and was used by no less a personage than the governor of one of our states in an election campaign. And while we are on the subject of politics, it would be well to note the delight and curiosity occasioned in 1952 by President Truman's revival of the term *snollygoster* (a near-nonsense word from frontier tall talk, meaning a pretentious boaster). Its appearance sent inquiring reporters to the dictionaries, and amateur etymologists to word lists of Pennsylvania Dutch.

In many literary works, such as Sinclair Lewis's *Elmer Gantry,* we find illustrations of the lay American attitude toward the verbally esoteric. Gantry, the revivalist of Lewis's bitterly satiric novel, asserts, "They make us work good and hard, Brother Jewkins. They give us pretty deep stuff: hermeneutics, chrestomathy, pericopes, exegesis, homiletics, liturgics, isagogics, Greek and Hebrew and Aramaic, hymnology, apologetics—oh, a good deal." And Lewis tells us that Mrs. Gantry "marveled to find Elmer even more profound than she had thought," and Elmer himself "reflected proudly that he really knew what all but a couple of the words meant." Such attitudes toward impressive words are still a characteristic of American English, even though widespread education since World War II has made the average American perhaps a little less gullible about polysyllabic words.

In the preceding chapter considerable space was given to those words which in American English have retained a meaning once current in England but which have since died out or changed there. Frequently, of course, the reverse occurred: new meanings were developed in this country, and many of these are traceable to the development of American institutions and American ways of life.

Not infrequently words have acquired a broader meaning in the United States than they had in England. *Freight* offers an excellent example of this type of change. In England it is applied only to merchandise transported by water, and as such it bears a relationship to the word *fraught,* "laden." Early in the nineteenth century *freight* came to be applied in the United States to merchandise dispatched overland as well, quite possibly because long-distance shipping from one part of the country to another often involved hauling by land as well as by water. Transporting a load of goods from New York to St. Louis, for example, around 1840 might well have involved river packet, canal boat, short railroad hauls, and pack train.

American politics, particularly in the rough-and-tumble days of Jacksonian democracy and the boss-ridden atmosphere of the post-Civil War era, appears to have given the word *politician* an unfavorable connotation. The *Oxford English Dictionary* definition of the term, satisfactorily explicit on this point, unconsciously reveals another British-American difference in terminology. It reads, "One keenly interested in politics; one who engages in party politics or in political strife, or who makes politics his profession or business; also (especially in the U.S.) in a sinister sense, one who lives by politics *as a trade."*

It is safe to say that this contrast between a profession or business on the one hand and a trade on the other as a means of elucidating the less favorable meaning of *politician* in the United States would never have occurred to an American lexicographer. In fact, the definition amuses any American who comes upon it simply because the hierarchy or ranking order which is implicit here has little significance in his scale of social values. It does serve as a reminder, however, that the verb *trade* in the sense of "to shop" or "to purchase regularly" (I always trade at Brown & Dobson's) is so purely American that it was not recorded by the *Oxford English Dictionary,* whose editorial staff and readers may well have been unaware of it, nor by the dictionaries of Americanisms, for whose editors it may have been so obvious and familiar that it was overlooked. It clearly developed out of the prevalence of bartering in a frontier society. Furthermore, there was a widespread use of *swap* as the general term meaning "exchange," facilitating the specialization of the other word. As a final chapter, the

American practice of purchasing cars, refrigerators, washing machines, and other durable goods by turning in an older article of the same kind, usually in lieu of a down payment, has given rise to *trade-in,* used both as verb and noun.

Back in the realm of politics, the originally innocent term *junket* has undergone pejoration. The word originally meant a basket and first appears in English in 1382. A century later it was applied to a dessert of sweetened curds, then to any cake or confection, and finally to a feast or banquet. From this last meaning, the verb *to junket* was created in the middle of the sixteenth century. This verbal use apparently formed the basis of the American political term which means to take a trip at public expense, ostensibly for purposes of legislative investigation or fact-finding, for the verbal noun *junketing* is recorded as early as 1809, the agentive *junketer* in 1862, and finally the noun itself in 1886.

Whereas *politician* and *junket* lost caste in American English because of circumstances peculiar to the development of our institutions, certain other words have acquired more favorable meanings. *Lumber,* already discussed in connection with functional change, also serves as a striking instance of amelioration. In England, *lumber* ordinarily indicates anything that takes up room or is left lying about, and the lumber room in a house is the one to which discarded toys, unwanted or unused wedding presents, empty trunks and the like are relegated.

That this meaning was brought to America is evident from its survival in some local dialects as well as from a good deal of early legislation. The *Boston Records* for 1663 show that the inhabitants were cautioned to "take care that noe wood, logges, timber, stonnes, or any *other* lumber be layed upon the flatte to the annoyance of any vesselles," and a similar law was passed in 1701 against encumbering any street, lane, or alley. Certainly in a pioneer community with building going on constantly, cut timber would inevitably be piled in the streets from time to time, and the circumstance that this was so often the offending impediment seems to have led to a specific association of *lumber* with cut or milled wood, in contrast to uncut logs or possibly standing trees, as is suggested by the report of Sir Edmund Andros, written in 1678: "The Comodityes of the Country to ye westward are wheat . . . pipe staves, timber, lumber & horses." *Lumber* as a noun meaning "cut or milled logs" has given rise to a host of compound formations, *lumberjack* being but one example.

The verb *haul* has similarly undergone a kind of amelioration in American English. In England the word generally suggests a considerable exertion of force or violence; in America it is used very often as a synonym for *drawing* or *carting.* Whether pioneer conditions, particularly with respect to roads, made transportation so difficult that a great expenditure of force was necessary at all times, or whether the American tendency toward hyperbole tended to make a "haul" of an ordinary carting task is difficult to say, but as early as 1714 we find a New Hampshire will stipulating, "I give to my sons . . . all materials of iron for hauling, plowing, and such like." Later on we find the word employed particularly in connection with railroad transportation and then apparently changing to a noun in the combination *long-* and *short-haul,* not to mention *U-Haul* trucks and car trailers; but it should be pointed out that British English developed *haulage* in this same connection as early as 1826.

The freedom with which certain English lexical patterns were treated in America reflects the frontier independence of spirit and lack of regard for accepted tradition. This is particularly evident in our many compound formations, our word blends, and our creation of mouth-filling terms. Certain changes, chiefly in meaning, have come about more gradually, and they too are new creations in a very real sense, answering to the slow but nevertheless inevitable development of American institutions and conditions under which the American people lived.

It is important, however, to realize that innovation, whether it is evidenced in the form of a word, its grammatical function, or its meaning, is but one of the processes which operated to make American English what it is today. Too often, in considerations of this general subject, innovation is stressed to the exclusion of other forces which are of equal significance but possibly somewhat less dramatic. Nor should we overlook the fact that the innovations which have been discussed in this chapter are almost totally confined to the area of vocabulary, including derivation and semantic extension. What is characteristically American in pronunciation is to be accounted for more often on the basis of retention of older features of the language, and as we have already seen, departures from British English in inflection and syntax are relatively few. Yet the most striking feature of American English innovations is their close correspondence to the temperament and life styles of those people who developed them.

6

The Rise and Fall
of the Genteel Tradition

Innovation is not tied exclusively to the free life of the frontier, rowdiness, or any other single characteristic. As settlement proceeded throughout most of the nineteenth century, each new wave of population contributed its own creation of original compounds. At the very time that the restless woodsman and trapper was making his initial foray into that portion of the wilderness farthest in advance of the march of civilization, the territory one or two hundred miles behind him was taking on the aspects of permanent settlement. Farms were established in the clearings or on the prairie; shipping points became the nuclei from which villages developed; local government, schools, churches, and even libraries soon took on at least a rudimentary form of organization. Even the theater and the lecture tours known as the lyceum course were seldom far behind the woodman's axe. They brought with them a decorum that is more directly reflected in the lexicon than is the free-spiritedness of the cowboy and the mountain man.

Probably the reflection of frontier life and institutions, the absence of certain restraints associated with more permanent types of civilization, the ingenuity born of sheer necessity made their mark on the language; but there is more to the story than just this. Other ramifications of pioneer civilization and indeed certain counter-movements or reactions against it must be taken into consideration as well if we are to comprehend the development of American English in its totality.

Settlers who had come from cities and towns which had acquired stability and certain cultural accoutrements permitted their imaginations to clothe their drab and commonplace surroundings with the salient features of the life they had known. One striking illustration of this tendency may be found in the peculiarly American development of the word *saloon,* the equivalent of British English *public house.* This word was originally an early-eighteenth-century adaptation of French *salon,* and at the time it was borrowed signified just what it has continued to mean in French, namely, a drawing room. Not long after its adoption it came to be applied to drawing rooms which were particularly large and elegant, often those of a public character. This association with elegance and fashion has remained unchanged in British English—witness the coinage *saloon car* for an automobile with an enclosed body.

The first coinage, in the United States, for the place where alcoholic spirits were drunk—the ultimate meaning of *saloon*—was *bar-room,* which is recorded by a British traveler as early as 1809. Indirect evidence suggests that the new term was insufficiently elegant to be wholly satisfactory, nor did *groggery,* which appeared just a little later, seem to constitute an acceptable improvement. About three decades later we find *saloon* appearing first on the eastern seaboard and then spreading westward with amazing rapidity. Whether this was a direct adaptation of the term in America, or whether its use was first suggested by the English *saloon bar*—the most elegant of the three types of bar in a public house, the other two being the private and the public bar—cannot be determined from the evidence currently available. The important thing, however, is that a word previously associated with fashion, elegance, and politeness came to be used in connection

120 AMERICAN ENGLISH

with a kind of establishment which was often fairly mean and
dingy—and which was still frequently designated by the much less
elegant term *bar*. Consequently, *saloon* suffered in status, and underwent pejoration.

As the agitation against the sale and use of alcohol increased,
the Anti-Saloon League was organized, and the saloon became a
symbol of corruption and evil influence. One of the principal aims
of the Prohibition movement was to wipe out the saloon, and although it failed after a decade and a half, and liquor eventually
came back, Mencken's comment that, "So far as I know, there is
not a simple undisguised saloon in the United States today," is still
essentially correct. Nor is the owner of such an establishment any
longer content to refer to himself as a saloonkeeper. The bar-
tender, too, has often attempted to cloak his occupation with a
new word, but the campaign, instituted in 1901 by the *Police
Gazette,* to substitute *bar clerk* or *mixologist* as an occupational
term had no success.

In all this, however, what is significant is the attempt to lend
dignity and attractiveness through the use of a new and somewhat
elegant word—more elegant, perhaps, than the situation would
reasonably permit.

A similar development occurred in connection with the term
opera house, but unfortunately little factual information concerning its use is available in the usual lexicographical sources. Nevertheless, throughout the nineteenth century and continuing on into
the twentieth, it seems to have been customary in many small
towns to use this word for the theater or auditorium which served
the community. Most of the opera houses scattered throughout
the length and breadth of the land seldom witnessed any perfor-
mance even remotely resembling an opera, except possibly for an
occasional venture into Gilbert and Sullivan by the local high
school. Robert and Helen Lynd, in their cultural analysis of Mun-
cie, Indiana, *Middletown,* list the following as opera-house sensa-
tions of the 'nineties: *The Telephone Girl, Over the Garden Wall,
East Lynne, Guilty Without Crime, The Black Crook,* and the in-

evitable *Uncle Tom's Cabin*. It would seem, therefore, that *opera house* as a term for the small-town American theater represents precisely the same tendencies, cultural and semantic, that were behind the adoption of *saloon* for a drinking establishment: a desire to make the ordinary seem somewhat grander than it actually was, coupled perhaps with the hope that some day the structure might come to justify the name given to it.

These tendencies were certainly operative during the formative period of American English, but the situation is greatly different today and a term like *opera house* seems quaintly old-fashioned. Perhaps the major survival of the older term is in *Grand Ole Op'ry*, the term for a country music program on radio and television.

Many terms manifesting this same tendency are to be observed in connection with our educational institutions and various types of training schools. In fact, there is if anything a double impulse here. The first is to be found in the tendency to dignify academic institutions of all kinds with a name that is a degree above, or at best somewhat more impressive than, that which they would merit in England. An obvious example is what has happened to the word *college*. A telling illustration of how this tendency operates is furnished by the state of Michigan where, in the decade of the 1930's, all but one of the normal schools in the state officially became Colleges of Education and in the 'fifties dropped the prepositional modifier. This change was officially justified by the establishment in each school of a liberal arts curriculum leading to the bachelor's degree, but the fact remains that *college* clearly seemed to the educational authorities a more desirable and respectable term than *school*. That *university* underwent a similar extension for much the same reason is evident from the exultant statement of a misguided patriot of the 1870's: "There are two universities in England, four in France, ten in Prussia, and thirty-seven in Ohio." Even *high school,* the American use of which dates from 1824, is seldom used for a secondary school in England, and in Europe it regularly denotes an institution of college or university rank. Here, however, American usage may have had its roots in Scotland.

The second tendency is to apply to trade schools and other establishments devoted to the training of artisans the same labels which have in the past been reserved for academic institutions. Again evidence is scanty, but *business college* as a term for a stenographic and secretarial training venture, is to be found as early as 1865. The dictionaries are strangely silent on *barber college,* but it was current in parts of the United States early in the twentieth century. Its sister institutions, the schools and colleges of cosmetology, devoted to initiating the beginner into the mysteries of the permanent wave, probably do not go back beyond the 1920's.

Occupational terminology, whether academic or not, has undergone a series of changes quite similar to those which have already been observed: old terms have been extended in application; new ones have been created. The words *doctor* and *professor* are obvious instances of extensions in application. Both of these are carefully restricted in their use in England, where surgeons are *Mr.* even if they do hold the M.D. degree, and professorships are naturally much less numerous than in the United States. In America, dentists, osteopaths, chiropractors, optometrists, chiropodists, and veterinarians are all doctors, and in addition the tremendous extension of the doctorate in American graduate schools and the lavish manner in which American colleges and universities distribute honorary degrees add to the number of doctors on other levels as well. Even so, this does not take into account such jocular applications, either in full form or the clipped *Doc,* which, as the *Dictionary of Americanisms* indicates, was extended to logging camps late in the nineteenth century. In the Black community, the use of (*hoodoo* or *voodoo*) *doctor* has extended to talented practitioners in any field, notably "Dr. J." (Julius Erving) of basketball fame.

Professor has developed in much the same direction; in fact, it may have begun earlier if it did not go so far. We find an enterprising bookseller styling himself a Professor of Book Auctioneering as early as 1774, and virtually every attempt at a glossary of Americanisms during the nineteenth century mentions the extension of the title to such groups as dancing teachers, magicians, and phrenologists. Certainly in most small towns the title was regularly applied to not only superintendents of schools and principals but even male grade-school teachers. The result of this wholesale doctoring and professoring is, on occasion, an avoidance of the titles by those who are normally entitled to them, an outcome suggested by the mock-serious society organized at the University of Virginia "for the encouragement of the use of *mister* to all men, professional or otherwise."

A familiar instance of the process of extension drawn from the vocabulary of college life is the word *fraternity*. The word is first recorded in English in 1330, applied to a religious order, and in 1386 to members of trade guilds and similar companies. The more strictly etymological meanings of brotherhood and brotherliness also appear in due course.

In this country within six months after the Declaration of Independence, a group of students at William and Mary College organized a literary society which they labeled cryptically with the three Greek letters Phi, Beta, and Kappa. The oath of membership pledged them to secrecy as to the significance of the name, to the pursuit of learning, and to eternal brotherhood. Because of this last, the organization became known as a fraternity. In due course similar societies followed, called themselves fraternities, and ultimately the term became definitely associated with collegiate organizations, social and professional as well as honorary, and even with similar groups in the secondary schools. The development of a specifically American institution gave the word a special application which it never acquired in England.

Nor did the process stop here. The development of women's colleges and of co-education gave rise to similar women's organizations; consequently a complementary specialization of the word *sorority* is to be found at the beginning of the present century, but even before this the term *fraternity,* despite its masculine derivational meaning, was extended to some women's groups, a number of which proudly retain it to this day. Americans were never much aware of the masculine feature in *frater-;* during World War II, orders were frequently given against "fraternizing" with the occupants of a war zone. One popular cartoon showed a furious sergeant bellowing at a bespectacled private: "Whaddya mean, Latin derivation? Of course it applies to women!"

As these societies, loosely associated with educational institutions, developed traditions and modes of behavior, a whole new vocabulary grew up, bringing with it such further changes in meaning as are to be found in the terms *pledge, pledging,* and *rushing*—to say nothing of the phrase *pinning a girl*—such compounds as *fraternity pin, fraternity house, fraternity brother,* the clipped form *frat,* and the derivative *rushee.* A somewhat similar account might be written about the American development of fraternal orders as applied to groups which bear such startling names as Moose, Elks, Eagles, and Red Men.

Another instance of a special meaning that developed as a result of conditions peculiar to American educational life is *sabbatical,* referring to a professorial holiday granted every seventh year. Even in universities, however, a "sabbatical" may sometimes be given after three or four years. In the business world, a "sabbatical" is sometimes used for any kind of extended leave of absence given to a fairly high-ranking executive.

Many of these terms are obviously related to the American passion for inflated designations. The process is characteristic of many occupations. *Mortician,* frequently thought of in this connection, appears to have been created about 1895 on the convenient analogy of *physician,* and the same process of derivation has given us *beautician* and six or eight others, all somewhat bizarre. It is possible that *mortician* may owe its creation quite as much to the age-old and constant search for euphemisms for terms associated with death and burial as to the desire for professional status. There is, after all, a somewhat gruesome pun in the word *undertaker,* and though it has served the English from 1698 on, they do at times soften the effect by substituting *funeral furnisher.*

Realtor, another oft-cited instance of the American creation of pseudo-professional terms, could be excused by the generously inclined on the ground that it permitted a single word to replace the somewhat cumbersome *real-estate agent,* but there is probably more truth than fiction in the sentiment expressed by Sinclair Lewis's Babbitt to the effect that, "We ought to insist that folks call us 'realtors' and not 'real-estate men'. Sounds more like a reg'lar profession." Though the Lewis citation comes from the early 1920's, the term itself dates from 1915.

American regard for technology is shown by the overwhelming popularity of the word *engineer,* used in strange and numerous combinations. Our early use of the term in connection with railroading was a portent of things to come; the English in general content themselves with the somewhat more humdrum-sounding *engine driver.* But since that time we have employed the word in an astounding number of combinations, running to well over 2000. H. L. Mencken reported that the *Extermination Engineers,* namely the rat and roach eradicators, had a national association for some thirty years. Such further terms as *patent engineer, recreation engineer, erosion engineer,* and *casement window engineer* illustrate the variety of uses to which the term has been put.

The proposal of a Janitor's Institute, held at Mt. Pleasant, Michigan, in 1939, to the effect that janitors henceforth be called *engineer-custodians,* reveals as well the temporary nature of the satisfaction to be derived from verbal glorification, for historically *janitor* represents quite the same state of mind that gave rise to *realtor* and *mortician.* Derived somewhat artificially from the mythological character Janus, it was first used for a doorkeeper or porter, and its application to the sweeper of floors and builder of fires has been confined primarily to the United States; in England *caretaker* is the common term. As is evident from the action of the institute, even forty years ago the word had become sufficiently tarnished that *engineer, custodian,* or both, sounded more attractive. One of the amusing sequels of the shift in terminology from *janitor* to *custodian* in one American university was that the title of the head of a research library had, in turn, to be changed from *Custodian* to *Director,* since there was some danger of confusing him with the janitor of the place.

This tendency to glorify the commonplace was not limited to the professional and work-a-day worlds. The American household bears some marks of this, even today. In the early 1920's and 1930's it was considered proper, particularly by women, to refer to the evening meal (*supper,* to the old-fashioned) as *dinner. Luncheon,* for the same speakers, in turn replaced *dinner* as the designation of the midday meal.

This shift is a slightly delayed reflection of the changed eating habits of many American families which developed from the increased urbanization and industrialization of the country. For the farming and small-town families at the beginning of the present century, the heaviest meal of the day was served at noon, and the evening repast was considerably lighter. Thus for that time, *dinner* and *supper* were accurate descriptions. The present tendency toward lighter meals at noon, frequently consumed away from the home by the working members of the family and by the children, has resulted in the heavier meal being served at home in the evening, with a resultant change in terminology and a prestige-loss for *supper.*

In this connection it is interesting to observe that *supper* not only continued in common use in America some sixty or seventy years longer than in England, but that this was a matter for comment by at least two mid-nineteenth-century British travelers. In 1859, Gosse in a series of letters from Alabama wrote, "The meal which we are accustomed to call 'tea' is by Americans universally, I believe, called 'supper,' and it is the final meal, there being but three in the day." Five years later we find C. Geithe reporting, "I chatted . . . till tea, or as they called it, supper."

As American domestic architecture has changed, so too have the names given to the various rooms. The principal phenomenon over the past century has been the disappearance of a "best room," rarely occupied on weekdays and used only to entertain guests and for holidays or festive occasions. In American usage this was the *parlor*. This in itself was a shift from British English, where the term *parlor* was applied to a rather small intimate chamber, whereas the more pretentious one was called the *drawing room*, a term which never caught on with Americans. In the United States, as long as the parlor was an institution, the room which was ordinarily used by the family circle was the *sitting room*, but as the parlor disappeared, the sitting room became the *living room*, and the former term came to be felt as somewhat rustic and old-fashioned.

It may be noted that only in America was the term *cuspidor*, adopted from Portuguese through Dutch, applied to what was at one time a common accessory in the home, to say nothing of the clubrooms and legislative halls. This somewhat delicate word was also introduced into England as early as 1781 but never gained any real currency there. For other words reflecting Portuguese-Dutch transmission and their importance to American English, see pp. 49–51.

Finally, the tendencies toward verbal elegance and sentimentality appear to have combined to produce a more extensive use of *home* in America than in England. At the close of the last century, George Warrington Steevens commented, "As to the home, the American talks about it a great deal. He never builds himself a house; he builds himself a home." Consequently, contractors for domestic dwellings are *home builders*, the householder is a *homeowner*, vacuum cleaners, dishwashing machines, garbage disposals, ice makers, microwave ovens, and the other manifold mechanical appurtenances of the American household are *home appliances*. School instruction in cooking and sewing has become *homemaking*, and when exalted to a more learned level, *home economics*. Even the housewife became a *homemaker* by formal resolution of the Long Island Federation of Women's Clubs, as Mencken pointed out. Moreover, the institutions of refuge for the needy, and those of detention for troublesome juveniles are quite regularly *homes*, to say nothing of *funeral homes*, which customarily serve as the setting for final rites, and *nursing homes,* as places of residence for increasing numbers of our old people.

Travelers to America, almost from the very beginning as an independent country, have taken great delight in pointing out what seemed to them a fundamental inconsistency between the theory of equality upon which the government of the country is based and the fondness of the American people for titles of honor. Although Crèvecoeur, reflecting on his pre-Revolutionary experience, stoutly insisted that *lawyer, merchant,* and *farmer* were the fairest titles our country at that time afforded, observers from the 1840's on have a quite different story to tell. As late as 1896, George Warrington Steevens inquired somewhat petulantly in describing the American, "Why does he cling all his life to the title of some rank or office he held twenty years ago?" Two answers to the question were offered some years before Steevens phrased it, and without question there is some truth in each. In 1849, the Scotsman Alexander Mackay defended the Americans on the ground that, "the fondness for titles which they display is but a manifestation of the fondness for distinction natural to the human mind." A somewhat different opinion was voiced a decade later by Thomas Colley Grattan, who concluded, "Were a well-established, national self-reliance felt among the leading men in the United States, there would be none of the melancholy parodies of 'high life,' none of the yearnings after aristocratical distinctions which are now so flagrant."

When American honorifics are examined in a dispassionate light, it must be said that they are still a far cry from Teutonic usage, for example. They are notable chiefly for some extension of bogus military titles such as *Colonel,* the retention of legislative and judicial titles, and the somewhat comic extension of the word *Honorable.* Judged by either general European or Latin American standards in these matters, the English-speaking Americans become almost shrinking violets. It is only in the light of English practice that our use of honorifics seems somewhat overweighted.

As H. L. Mencken pointed out, the term *Honorable* is the most abused of our honorifics. The President and the members of his cabinet and the justices of the Supreme Court certainly merit the term, but our very concept of the equality of the three branches of government demands that all members of the Senate and the House of Representatives receive it as well. Then there arises the problem of appellate and district judges, to say nothing of under-secretaries and assistant secretaries. There is the whole diplomatic corps in addition, and officials in special government agencies not represented in the cabinet. Leaving the national government and pursuing the same problem on the state level, we must now multiply by fifty the possibly 2000 *Honorables* we have already conferred. The ludicrous size of the resultant list makes further comment unnecessary.

Euphemism, verbal prudery, or the avoidance of the unpleasant word, is another somewhat indirect product of the frontier which, from a semantic and lexical point of view at least, is often closely allied to verbal glorification. In fact, it is often difficult to decide whether the motive behind such a substitution as that of *casket* for *coffin* was primarily that of suggesting something more elegant or that of avoiding a term connected with death and burial. Much of the verbal prudery, however, for which we became notorious in the nineteenth century, may be traced to two factors: the position of women in American society and the predominantly middle-class character of American culture.

The second of these points does not require extensive elaboration. Within the history of modern societies it has always been the middle class which has manifested a greater and more anxious concern for the proprieties than either the lower class, which has tended toward indifference, or the upper, which has been protected by a thick coat of self-assurance. Among the proprieties thus affected, that of language has usually assumed a prominent position. It was the English middle class, or at least the upper sector of it, which created the demand which led to the extensive schoolmastering of the language in eighteenth-century England. That the Puritan settlers of New England—also predominantly

middle class—were intensely concerned with linguistic propriety is
indicated by the amount of colonial legislation directed against
profanity. Noah Webster interested himself in expurgating the
Bible, and considered this one of his important works. There is
ample evidence in a dozen sociological studies that most Americans are prone to think of themselves as belonging to the middle
class and consequently observing a multitude of linguistic taboos.

This was probably true until about 1960, when the movement
sometimes termed the counter-culture, in which youngsters (often
middle-class by most definitions of the term) calling themselves
"Hippies" (earlier, "Beats" or "Beatniks") imitated less conventional lifestyles, particularly that of the Black ghetto, and brought
into general use some terms that would have been shocking
twenty years—or even four or five years—earlier. In the last
twenty years there has been an astonishing change in the admissi-
bility of terms formerly considered obscene.

More recently, a change in the attitude of women has modified
not only the cherished American notion about who uses obscene
words, but also when, and where. In earlier centuries, and earlier
decades of the twentieth century, women were the chief influence
in promoting verbal delicacy. Because of women's scarcity value,
their accepted attitude toward language fostered an extreme sensi-
tivity in linguistic matters. In the 1970's, the Women's Liberation
movement has rejected, and at times even reversed, that attitude.

This has been only a small part, however, of the projected influence on language of the feminist movement. Some women have insisted upon certain vocabulary changes, so that *chairman* is now
often *chairperson* and *humankind* is sometimes used for *mankind*.
They also object to the use of the masculine third person singular
pronoun *he* in its standard, formal function of referring to any
person not determinably of female sex. Some writers now use *s/he*
or *she/he* as substitutes, and some academic style manuals now
recommend that usage. Perhaps best known, however, is the use
of *Ms.* (also the title of the first feminist magazine in the United

States) as a form of polite address to denote a woman, whether married or not. Feminists had observed that the man could list himself as *Mr.* without reporting on his marital status, and that women should be accorded the same privilege.

One finds it almost impossible, in 1980, to imagine the linguistic world which Captain Frederick Marryat reported on in the middle of the nineteenth century. He tells first of how he offended an American woman by saying *legs* instead of *limbs*. His account mentions the girls' seminary where the piano "limbs" were "dressed in modest little trousers with frills at the bottom of them." That the veracity of the latter story has been questioned is of little importance; it is true in spirit to the segment of American life it purported to reflect.

In language, questionable subjects like sex were, until recently, kept out of sight and mind (ostensibly if not actually), by developing new and less shocking terms to replace those which had taken on taboo characteristics. All languages do this to some extent. It is the degree to which these euphemistic tendencies operated in American English almost to the middle of the twentieth century, and how completely they have disappeared in the last ten years, that is of particular interest here.

One outlet for verbal delicacy of this nature was the creation of a host of thinly disguised terms for a house of prostitution. *Assignation house* is cited by the *Dictionary of Americanisms* for 1854; *house of assignation* preceded this by twenty years. *Sporting house,* which in England meant first merely a house frequented by sportsmen and later a gambling house, was finally applied to a brothel in America in 1894. None of the dictionaries, however, seem to record the use of *sport* for a prostitute, which was current about the same time. *Crib* also reflects the same transition from a gaming house to one of prostitution, though somewhat earlier, and such terms as *cat house, fancy house, cow bag,* and *call house* were all in use at one time or another. On a somewhat more dignified level, *disorderly house* and *house of ill fame* were perhaps the best-known terms. Things had changed so much, however, by the 1970's that Broadway could present a play entitled *The Best Little Whorehouse in Texas.*

Cadet as a euphemism for procurer seems to have flourished from the first to the third decades of the twentieth century. *Pimp* has come to be regarded as a less-than-shocking word in the last ten years or so; it was the title of a widely circulated autobiography by Robert Beck, alias Iceberg Slim. By now, several studies of ghetto pimps have found their way into even the most respectable bookstores.

There was also an equal reticence with respect to naming specific venereal diseases, but this has been generally overcome within the past forty years. During the World War II period, posters advertising the effects of penicillin on syphilis and gonorrhea were put up in public without arousing too much opposition to the sight of the formerly taboo words.

Another object which once invited euphemistic terminology is what the English call a *water closet* and the Americans a *toilet.* The first citation of *toilet* in its present American sense bears the date 1909, though it must have had this meaning considerably earlier. *Rest room* (1909) and *comfort station* (1904) were also concocted during the first decade of the century, and Mencken credits *powder room* to the speakeasies of the Prohibition era. The American use of *washroom* in the same sense goes back to 1853. *John* is, for some reason, regarded as being a more frank and derogatory term.

As an example of the former delicacy of usage for parts of the body, the taboo against *leg* was extended to fowl prepared for the table. However, *drumstick,* one of the euphemisms which appeared on the scene as a substitute, is clearly of British origin and on the basis of dictionary evidence, at least, was as much used in Britain as in the United States. The extension of *joint,* from its British use in connection with such meats as beef, mutton, and venison, to roast fowl seems clearly to have originated in America, and so too the further distinction between a first joint and a second. An English traveler to America in 1845 reported himself as being "requested by a lady, at a public dinner table, to furnish her with the first and second joint." The equally strong taboo against *breast,* coupled with that of *leg,* gave rise to another pair of American euphemisms used in this connection. Thomas C. Grattan, in his *Civilized America* (1859) explained that, "some . . . would scarcely hesitate, though almost all call it the 'white meat,' in contradistinction to the 'dark meat' as all ladies and gentlemen designate the legs of poultry." *White meat* as a term had previously existed in England, but was limited in its meaning to milk, cheese, and other dairy products, literally white food.

Undergarments for both men and women likewise offered a fertile field for mid-nineteenth-century ingenuity. *Unmentionables,* which refers at times to trousers and at others to drawers, is cited as early as 1839; *sub-trousers* as early as 1890. Between these dates a wide variety of terms appeared, though it should be noted that *inexpressibles,* sometimes classed with American euphemisms of this type, is actually British in origin and seems to have been used in England throughout the greater part of the century. As late as the 1950's, *panties* would have been considered an embarrassing word by some Americans; in the 1970's, the word was everywhere, and compounds like *control top pantyhose* are freely heard in commercials on television, even during "family viewing hours," when children are likely to be watching.

Old age, death, dying, and burial constitute another area of the lexicon in which most languages develop a large number of euphemisms. These particular taboos and the euphemisms they generate have not disappeared in the alleged sophistication of the 1970's and 1980's. *Nursing home* has all but replaced *old folks' home* (and *poorhouse,* for that matter); *social security, Medicare,* and *Medicaid* encompass most of our recent ideas of charity to the aging, who are *senior citizens* now rather than old people. *Casket,* which serves as a delicate substitute for *coffin,* seems to have entered the language by way of the compound *burial casket,* which along with *burial case* was coined in the 'fifties and 'sixties of the last century. It must have caught on very rapidly, for by 1870 a British news correspondent in New York was able to make the flat statement, "In America a coffin is called a casket." The perfumed practices of the modern mortician have, of course, resulted in a host of evasive expressions, which have been more lastingly effective than the sexual euphemisms in our late-twentieth-century era of alleged freedom of expression.

The Puritan prohibition of profanity has already been mentioned, and although the number of violations of their laws clearly indicates that this was more often honored in the breach than in the observance, yet the fact that the laws should have existed at all, as well as the length of time they remained on the books, offers satisfactory evidence of an active taboo against profanity in the Puritan conscience. As a consequence of this, it would seem, American English developed a whole lexicon of near-swearing, including *darn, drat, doggone, blasted, Sam Hill, gee whittaker, gee whiz,* and their progeny of sixty or seventy others, most of them bearing more or less phonetic resemblance to the particular morsel for which they were substituted. This particular taboo was so strong that when Rhett Butler's, "Frankly, darling, I don't give a damn" was actually heard from the moving picture screen in *Gone With the Wind,* 1938, moviegoers were shocked and titillated. By now, however, *damn* along with other words and expressions once even more strongly tabooed are familiar even in the popular media. The near-swearings of the past seem inexpressibly quaint in the 1970's and early 1980's.

It is important to recognize that taboos and the resulting euphemisms have always operated in language. We have had them in English from the time that some Anglo-Saxon monk with an over-keen sense of propriety, and a distinctly worldly knowledge of harbor resorts, coined the term *port-cwene* (port woman) to translate "harlot" in the parable of the Prodigal Son, up to the present era when all of our recent governmental administrations have been careful to characterize a slight economic depression as a *recession.* The interesting aspect of the mid-nineteenth-century development of euphemisms in America lies in the peculiar combination of cultural circumstances which brought it about, the lavish scale upon which it operated, and the extremes which it often attained.

Every movement has its counter-force, and the genteel tradition of the past was no exception. Nineteenth-century America was not without those individuals who not only accepted their lack of culture and refinement as an established fact but who gloried in it, and indeed flaunted it. The extreme of such an attitude has sometimes been called the "mucker pose," one which certain politicians and others dependent upon large-scale popular support have at times found it profitable to adopt. In the 1970's, especially in that area of popular music in which rock-and-roll gave way to "punk rock," the attitude had had a tremendous commercial success with teenagers. Linguistically, the mucker pose is frequently manifested by the conscious employment of features of nonstandard English; though there is also, at times, a genuine identification with the "disadvantaged" and ethnic populations who tend to use such dialects most naturally.

7

Social and Regional Variation

The English language is spoken natively in America by some two hundred million people, over an area of more than three million square miles, with a large number of minority sub-cultures offering proof that the "melting pot" was an ideal rather than a reality. For many groups found in all parts of the country, English is by no means the only—or even the first—language. Dialectologists are slowly coming to the realization that both class distribution of language variants, and prejudice against the users of "nonstandard" dialects are realities in twentieth-century America. Black English, the dialect of "disadvantaged" Black children, was recognized legally by a landmark Detroit court decision in July, 1979. Social dialect study was largely the product of the 1960's, but public awareness of social dialects may actually come about during the 1980's.

A pioneering sociologist, Glenna Ruth Pickford, began in 1956 to direct our attention to sociological factors like occupation and urban residence rather than to purely geographic factors in a paper published in that year but hardly noticed for ten years or so thereafter. The field of linguistics was, however, branching out

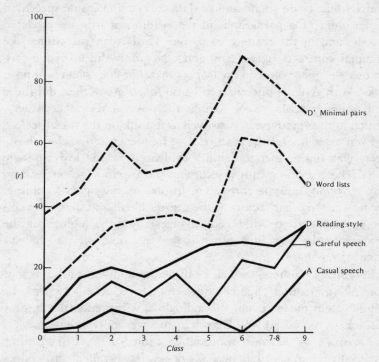

Detailed style stratification of (r): Nine Classes.
From William Labov's *Social Stratification of English in New York City.*
Reprinted by permission of the *Center for Applied Linguistics.*

into "hyphenated" disciplines like socio-linguistics, and works like William Labov's *Social Stratification of English in New York City* (1965), (though preceded by some important work on caste dialect in India), were perhaps most directly responsible for the new emphasis on social variation.

Labov's influential work, although it contains much more highly technical data, is best known for its demonstration that certain variables of pronunciation like *that* and *dat* or *fourth floor* "with or without [r]" are socially and contextually distributed. Labov demonstrated that every speaker has some differing pronunciations: to do so, he ranked data collected in casual speech, in the reading of a paragraph, in the reading of lists of unrelated words, and in the reading of paired words with something like minimal contrasts (*guard* and *god*). Not only did everyone pronounce "r" more often in the last context, but floorwalkers at posh Saks' Fifth Avenue put more "r" into *fourth floor* than did those at middle-class Macy's. S. Klein's, the poor man's haberdashery, trailed in the amount of "r" as well as in rank on the social scale.

Even more interesting than relative frequency across class, however, was the greater variability evidenced by the lower-middle class. These sociologically insecure people also indulge extensively, Labov found, in hypercorrection. Insofar as class goes (ignoring, for now, such other factors as the greater likelihood that a new biological generation will make changes), not the highest or the lowest but the class in between is the one most likely to foment linguistic change.

Research by others, as well as by Labov himself, indicates that *Social Stratification* slightly under-emphasized social factors like ethnic group membership. Black English, with many of the same features in New York and Detroit as in Shreveport, Louisiana, has become one of the most thoroughly studied dialects of all time. Especially prominent has been work on the so-called zero copula (*He my main man*), and the demonstration that all speakers who use the "zero" also realize the copula in some positions (*Yes, he is*), and that non-use of the verbs *is* and *are* is not categorical with any speaker. Labov's 1969 paper on this feature developed the theory of inherent variability, with variable rules becoming the indispensable new tool of variation studies. Almost overlooked, unfortunately, were the grammatical implications of Black English forms like preverbal *been* (*You been know dat; He been ate de chicken*) marking a strongly past time (longer ago, for example, than *He done ate de chicken*).

Dialectology, before the criticism expressed by sociologist Glenna Ruth Pickford, followed the reconstructive lead of the *Atlas Linguistique de la France* and the *Sprachatlas des Deutschen*

Reichs. The approach still dominates publications like the *Journal of English Linguistics* and *American Speech*. The nineteenth century had seen the beginning of the English Dialect Society (and publications like the *English Dialect Dictionary*), and the American Dialect Society was organized in 1889. Beginning in 1928, a group of researchers under the direction of Professor Hans Kurath undertook the compilation of a *Linguistic Atlas of the United States and Canada*. The *Linguistic Atlas of New England* was published over the period from 1939 to 1943. Considerably more field work has been completed since that time.

Pickford strongly criticized this work for including only three social groups (five in the closely related *Dictionary of American Regional English*) and for limiting, in practice, the interviews almost exclusively to rural informants. In the 1960's, partly in response to Pickford's criticism, dialectologists began to conduct studies in Washington, D.C., Detroit, Chicago, and New York.

From the Atlas research procedures there seemed to emerge three major dialect boundaries, cutting the country into lateral strips and labeled by Kurath: Northern, Midland, and Southern. (See the accompanying map.) This regional distribution had no place for either what Mencken had called the "American Vulgate" or for what others had called General American. Standardizing practices, often associated with the concept of General American, were dismissed as not really part of the informants' "natural" language.

What emerged in the dialect research of the 1960's, however, was something other than a picture of regional distribution. The "neutral" dialect concept of General American was replaced, especially in the research of certain psycholinguists, by that of Network Standard, the speech of television newscasters on the major networks and the kind of English which Americans clearly admired more than any other. They tended, however inaccurately, to form mental pictures of their own speech in terms of that prestige form. This regionally and socially neutral dialect clearly emerged as the ideal, if not the actuality, for most speakers of American

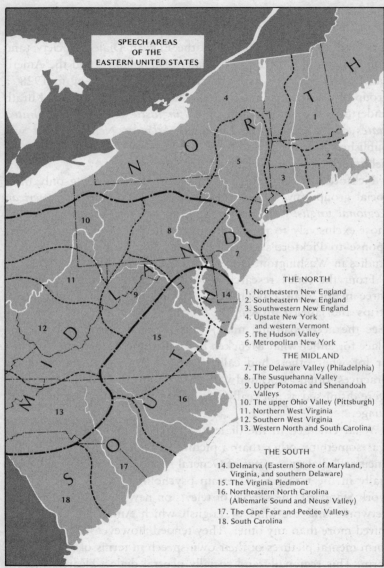

SPEECH AREAS
OF THE
EASTERN UNITED STATES

N O R T H

N O R T H

M I D L A N D

S O U T H

THE NORTH

1. Northeastern New England
2. Southeastern New England
3. Southwestern New England
4. Upstate New York
   and western Vermont
5. The Hudson Valley
6. Metropolitan New York

THE MIDLAND

7. The Delaware Valley (Philadelphia)
8. The Susquehanna Valley
9. Upper Potomac and Shenandoah
   Valleys
10. The upper Ohio Valley (Pittsburgh)
11. Northern West Virginia
12. Southern West Virginia
13. Western North and South Carolina

THE SOUTH

14. Delmarva (Eastern Shore of Maryland,
    Virginia, and southern Delaware)
15. The Virginia Piedmont
16. Northeastern North Carolina
    (Albemarle Sound and Neuse Valley)
17. The Cape Fear and Peedee Valleys
18. South Carolina

This map is taken from Hans Kurath's *Word Geography of the Eastern United States*, and is reproduced by permission of the *University of Michigan Press*.

English. Television, becoming really important as a medium in the 1960's, would permit relatively "nonstandard" usage from comedians and sportcasters, but anyone else had to disguise his dialect in order to work regularly for the networks. A nationally oriented and highly mobile population substituted this concept of a standard dialect for the older notion of prestige centers.

The older, geographically oriented type of research identified dialect areas for the essentially rural population in terms of predominantly lexical materials. For example, characteristic Northern expressions that were current throughout the area include *pail, swill, whiffletree* or *whippletree, comforter* or *comfortable* for a thick quilt, *brook, co-boss* or *come-boss* as a cow call, *johnny-cake, salt pork,* and *darning needle* for a dragonfly. When one considers how few cattle are called in New York City, or how few Manhattanites see a dragonfly during the course of a day, one realizes how irrelevantly quaint and rustic some of this research came to seem.

In the Midland area one found *blinds* for roller shades, *skillet, spouting* or *spouts* for eaves, a *piece* for food taken between meals, *snake feeder* for dragonfly, *sook* as the call to calves, *armload* for an armful of wood; and one *hulled* beans when he took off the shells. A quarter *till* the hour was a typical Midland expression, as the elliptical *to want off,* or *out,* or *in.* The South had *lightwood* as the term for kindling, a *turn* of wood for an armful; stringbeans were generally *snap beans; low* was used for the sound cows make at feeding time; *hasslet* was the term for the edible inner organs of a pig, and *chittlins* for the small intestines. The last item above has now, of course, achieved nationwide spread in connection with the Black institution of soul food.

Sub-dialect areas were also found to have their characteristic forms. In coastal New England, for instance, *pigsty* was the normal term for a pig-pen, *bonny clapper* for curdled sour milk, *buttonwood* for a sycamore, and *pandowdy* for a cobbler type of dessert. Some Eastern Virginians still have *cuppin* for a cow pen, and *corn house* for a crib. *Lumber room* survives as the term for a storeroom. *Hopper grass* competed with the national term *grass-hopper,* and *batter bread* was used for a soft cornbread containing egg.

As far as the domains of the American lexicon which reflect regional differences are concerned, the matter is summarized in Kurath's *Word Geography,* where the author points out first of all that the vocabularies of the arts and sciences, of industries, commercial enterprises, social and political institutions, and even many of the crafts, are national in scope because the activities they reflect are organized on a national basis. He then goes on to say:

> Enterprises and activities that are regionally restricted have, on the other hand, a considerable body of regional vocabulary which, to be sure, may be known in other parts of the country, even if it is not in active use. The cotton planter of the South, the tobacco grower, the dairy farmer, the wheat grower, the miner, the lumberman, and the rancher of the West have many words and expressions that are strictly regional and sometimes local in their currency.

> Regional and local expressions are most common in the vocabulary of the intimate everyday life of the home and the farm—not only among the simple folk and the middle class but also among the cultured . . . Food, clothing, shelter, health, the day's work, play, mating, social gatherings, the land, the farm buildings, implements, the farm stocks and crops, the weather, the fauna and flora—these are the intimate concern of the common folk in the countryside, and for these things expressions are handed down in the family and the neighborhood that schooling and reading and a familiarity with regional or national usage do not blot out.

In other domains of the lexicon, social differences are more strikingly important. Americans have, from the first, identified themselves much more by occupation than by region, and early commentators made much of the "jargon" of groups like the trappers ("mountain men") and the cowboys. Groups as diverse as hoboes, prostitutes, and advertising men have their own peculiar terminology and phraseology. In particular, American Blacks have

had African or Afro-Creole survivals; these survivals came to national attention beginning around 1920, through the vocabulary
of jazz and blues musicians. White musicians and then American
teenagers made a shibboleth of the use of Black-associated
"slang," and British rock groups like the *Beatles* and the *Rolling
Stones* propagated it among the English youth.

It is not only in the vocabulary that one finds regional differences in American speech; there are pronunciation differences
as well. Throughout the Northern area, for example, the distinction between [o] and [ɔ] in such word pairs as *hoarse* and *horse*,
mourning and *morning*, is generally maintained; [s] regularly
occurs in *grease* (verb) and *greasy* and *root* is pronounced with the
vowel of *wood*. Within the Northern area such sub-dialects as
coastal New England and Metropolitan New York also show
many characteristic forms, although the extreme amount of variation found in the latter must not be forgotten. The treatment of
the vowel of *bird* is only one of these, and words of the *calf, pass,
path, dance* group constitute another. In the Midland area
speakers fail to distinguish between *hoarse* and *horse* in many
contexts. Rounding is characteristic of the vowels of *hog, frog,
log, wasp,* and *wash,* and in the last of these words an *r* often in-
trudes in the speech of the rural and old-fashioned. The vowels of
due and *new* will resemble that of *food* rather than that of *feud*. In
the South and in eastern New England, there is a tendency to
"lose" *r* except before vowels; but the former does not have the
pronounced *Cuber* (for *Cuba*) and *idear of it* which John F. Kennedy carried from Massachusetts to the presidency. *R* is also
"lost" in eastern New England and in New York City but not in
the Northern area generally. Words like *Tuesday, due,* and *new*
have a *y*-like glide preceding the vowel, and final [z] in *Mrs.* is the
normal form.

Black speakers have spread some characteristics usually
regarded as Southern, such as the use of the vowel sound of *pin*
and *tin* in *pen* and *ten,* to the Northern cities. *Dat* for *that,* and
occasionally *muvver* for *mother,* and *baf* for *bath* are also charac-

teristic of "disadvantaged" Blacks in all parts of the country. Many Blacks also have "injective" or "imploded" stops in initial position for *b* and *d*. This pronunciation has spread to the speech of some Southern whites who have been strongly influenced by Blacks, but otherwise it is unknown in the English-speaking world except in the Afro-Creole varieties.

Black English provides the greatest examples of syntactic variation, although there has been considerable argument among dialectologists as to the exact degree. Preverbal *been* and "zero copula" have already been mentioned. Most of the controversy, however, has centered on preverbal auxiliary *be* and the closely related copula use: *He be sick (all the time)* as opposed to *He sick (right now)* has been the standard contrast, although more detailed study shows that the distinction is more complicated than that. *He be joking,* or *He be sick* negates with *don't; He sick* or *He working* with *ain't.* A more specific present-time context can be achieved with *He not sick* or *He not working.*

Regional variation in inflectional forms and syntax at the most superficial level can also be found, especially among older, relatively uneducated groups. *Hadn't ought* is a characteristic Northern double modal; *might could* and *may can* were perhaps exclusively Southern until Black speakers carried them into the Northern cities. Verb forms associated with the North have *been see* as a past tense form, *clim* for "climbed," *wa'n't* for "wasn't," uninflected *be* in such expressions as "How be you?" (much more limited syntactically than the superficially similar Black English form), and the choice of the preposition *to* in *sick to his stomach.* Associated with the Midlands were *clum* for "climbed," *seen* for "saw," *all the further,* and *I'll wait on you.* Characteristic Southern expressions, excluding Black English influence, were *belongs to be, heern* for "heard," *seed* as the past tense of "to see," and *holp* for "helped."

However quaint and rustic some of these forms may seem, and however unfamiliar to many other speakers of American English, they have been used, so far unsuccessfully, in attempts to trace the settlement history, particularly of the earliest immigrants. It has been hypothesized that, of ten families of settlers gathered in any one place, two might well have spoken London English, while three or four others spoke one of the southeastern county dialects. There might also have been a couple of families speaking northern English and another two or three employing a western dialect.

What would have happened to this hypothetical dialect mix is another matter. Recent studies emphasize the way in which children are influenced more strongly by the language of their peers than by that of their parents. Even if the parents retained the old regional dialect unchanged—and sociolinguistic research questions whether this is ever completely the case—children of the second generation would level the differences. Whatever compromises between British local dialects were worked out at various points on the Atlantic Seaboard would be supplemented by borrowings from the Indians and from other language groups. Other population groups which had extensive contacts with the children of the British immigrants, like the Black slaves of the Southern states, would also have strongly influenced their language.

Judging by the reports of observers, these influences became especially noticeable about the beginning of the nineteenth century. At about the same time, other changes occurred which were to have a profound effect upon the language situation in America. First, the industrial revolution resulted in the growth of a number of industrial centers, uprooting a considerable proportion of the farm population and concentrating it in the cities. The development of the railroad and other mechanical means of travel increased greatly the mobility of the average person. The large-scale migrations westward also resulted in some resettlement and shifting, even among those who did not set out on the long trek. All of this would have resulted in a general abandonment of narrowly local speech forms in favor of fewer, more accessible, varieties— even if there had not been prior forces leading toward the same end.

Some local speech forms have remained even to the present day.

These are usually known as relics, particularly when they are distributed in isolated spots over an area rather than in concentration. *Open stone peach,* for example, is a relic for "freestone peach," occurring in Maryland. *Smurring up,* "getting foggy," survives as a relic in eastern Maine and more rarely on Cape Cod and Martha's Vineyard.

Even prior to the shifts in population and changes in culture pattern, certain colonial cities such as Boston, Philadelphia, and Charleston had acquired prestige by developing as centers of trade and immigration. They became socially and culturally outstanding, as well as economically powerful, thus dominating the areas surrounding them. As a consequence, local expressions and pronunciations peculiar to the countryside came to be replaced by new forms of speech emanating from these cosmopolitan centers. A fairly recent instance of this is to be found in the New England term *tonic* for soda water, practically co-extensive with the area served by Boston wholesalers.

Little if anything of this sort has ever been observed for the influence of New York City on any large surrounding area. Nevertheless, Madison Avenue's influence on the advertising phraseology of the nation, along with the importance of New York City for radio, television, and publication, must have had a general, widely diffused influence. It has been suggested that the "Brooklyn" dialect of popular stereotype, particularly with its pronunciation of *bird, shirt, thirty-third,* etc. (imprecisely believed to be like "oÿ" of *Floyd*) resembles that of the same working-class people in New Orleans and elsewhere along the Atlantic and Gulf seacoasts because of the trade connections, particularly in cotton, between New Orleans and New York City.

Nor was the general process of dialect formation by any means completed with the settlement of the Atlantic seaboard. As the land to the west came to be taken up in successive stages (for example, western New York, Michigan, Wisconsin in the North; southern Ohio, Indiana, and southern Illinois in the Midland area), the same mixtures of speech forms among the settlers were present at first, and the same linguistic compromises had to be worked out. Although virtually every westward-moving group had to work out some way of dealing with the foreign-language groups in its language contact picture, the specific nature of the groups encountered varied at each stage.

The same processes occurred in the interior South, in Texas, and later on in the Far West. The complete linguistic history of the United States depends upon the formulation of what happened in each of those areas. We know, for example, from both surviving forms and historical sources that the Western cowboys used faro and poker terms (*in hock, pass the buck, deal from the bottom of the deck, four flusher*), and occupational terms (*little dogies, break the string, hand* for "worker"), many of which moved back toward the East.

Such environmental factors as topography, climate, and plant and animal life also played their part in influencing the dialect of an area, just as they did in the general transplanting of the English language to America. The complexity and size of the network of fresh-water streams affect the distribution and meaning of such terms as *brook, creek, branch,* and *river*—not to mention *wash* and *bayou.* In parts of Ohio and Pennsylvania, for example, the term *creek* is applied to a much larger body of water than in Michigan. It is even more obvious that in those parts of the country where snow is a rarity or does not fall at all, there will be no necessity for terms to indicate coasting face down on a sled. It is not surprising that those areas of the country where cows can be milked outside, for at least part of the year, will develop a specific term for the place where this is done: witness *milk gap* or *milking gap* current in the Appalachians south of the James River. The wealth of terms for various types of fences throughout the country is again dependent, in part at least, on the material which is available for building them, be it stones, stumps, or wooden rails. It is equally obvious that nationwide technological terms for television, like *commercial, station break, prime time, talk show,* and *situation comedy* should be the same in all parts of the country. Neither is it surprising that the increasingly nationwide distribution of major sporting events should lead to uniformity in *Super Bowl, Number One* ("We're Number One!"), *playoff, World Series,* and a host of other terms.

Before the days of radio, television, and national magazine advertising, a new invention or development introduced into several parts of the country at the same time would acquire different names in various places. The baby carriage, for example, seems to have been a development of the 1830's and '40's, and this is the term which developed in New England. Within the Philadelphia trade area, however, the article became known as a *baby coach. Baby buggy* was adopted west of the Alleghenies and *baby cab* in other regions throughout the country.

Within the last four decades, the building of large, double-lane, limited-access automobile highways has been undertaken in all parts of the country. In the beginning, there were many regional differences: *parkways* in eastern New York, Connecticut, and Rhode Island; *turnpikes* in Pennsylvania, New Jersey, New Hampshire, Maine, Massachusetts, Ohio, and Indiana. (The fanciest highway in Florida, from Miami to Gainesville, is, however, now a turnpike.) In New York *thruway* is used for what are *expressways* in Michigan and *freeways* in California. For a while—in the late 1950's—these seemed like regionalisms in the making, but a generation of car travelers has learned them all and uses them now synonymously, now with some specialization.

It is of interest also to look at the dialect situation from the point of view of various words which are employed for the same concept in different parts of the country. One of the most interesting and instructive distributions is to be found in connection with the terms used for *earthworm.* This word is used by cultivated speakers in the metropolitan centers. *Angleworm* is the regional term in the North, *fishworm* in the Midland area, and *fishing worm* in the coastal South. *Fish bait* and *bait worm* occupy smaller areas within the extensive *fishworm* region, but are also distributed over a wide territory.

In addition, there have been a large number of local terms, many of them used principally by the older and less-educated inhabitants. The Merrimack Valley, in New Hampshire, and Essex County, Massachusetts, have *mud worm*. *Eace worm* is used in Rhode Island. *Angle dog* appears in upper Connecticut, and *ground worm* on the Eastern Shore of Virginia. *Red worm* is used in the mountains of North Carolina, and an area around Toledo, Ohio, uses *dew worm*. Scattered instances of *rainworm* appear on Buzzards Bay in Massachusetts, throughout the Pennsylvania German area, and in German settlements in North Carolina, Maine, and Wisconsin. We have, thus, a wealth of older local terms, three distinct regional words, and the cultivated *earthworm* appearing in addition as a folk word in South Carolina and along the North Carolina and Virginia coast. Where and how did the various terms originate, and what can be determined about their subsequent history?

Earthworm itself is not an old word; it appears to have been compounded only shortly before the earliest English migrations to America. The earliest *Oxford English Dictionary* citation of the word in its present form is 1591; it appears also as *yearth worm* some thirty years earlier. The three regional terms all seem to have been coined in America; the dictionaries either record no British citations or fail to include the words at all.

The local terms have a varied and interesting history. *Mud worm* seems to occur in standard British English from the beginning of the nineteenth century on. *Eace worm,* as a combined form, goes back at least to Middle English; the first element was a term for "bait" as early as Aelfric; it is used today in a number of southern counties in England from Kent to Gloucester. *Angle dog* is used currently in Devonshire. *Ground worm,* though apparently coined in England, was transferred to North Carolina and Maryland in the eighteenth century. *Red worm* appears first in England in 1450 and continues through to the mid-nineteenth century, though chiefly in books on fishing, as does *dew worm,* which goes back even farther, to the late Old English period. *Rainworm,* though it appears in Aelfric as *renwyrm,* may be a re-formation, even in British English, on the pattern of *Regenwurm* in German, for there is a gap of seven centuries in the citations in the *Oxford English Dictionary* and there is reason to believe that its revival in 1731 was influenced by the German form. Moreover, with but one exception, it has been cited for the United States only in areas settled by Germans.

Thus we have in the standard cultivated term one of relatively recently British formation. Apparently the regional terms were compounded in America, whereas the local terms represent survivals either of dialect usage or anglers' jargon and one loan translation. It is worth noting that the common Old English term, *angle twicce,* surviving as *angle twitch* in Cornwall and Devon, seems not to have found its way to America. There are, furthermore, such other English formations as *tag worm, marsh worm,* and *garden worm* which have not been recorded in America.

At times, too, changes in meaning seem to have entered into the dialect situation, as is illustrated by the development of the regional terms *skillet* and *spider,* the former current in the Midland and the Virginia Piedmont, the latter in the North and the Southern Tidewater area. *Frying pan* is the urban term and is slowly supplanting the others. *Spider,* once a nautical term for "the iron band around the mast to take the lower end of futlock rigging," was then applied to a cast-iron pan with short legs. It was later transferred to the flat-bottomed pan as well. The local term *creeper* is used in Marblehead, Massachusetts. *Skillet,* a term of doubtful etymology, first appears in English in 1403, when it was applied to a long-handled brass or copper vessel used for boiling liquids or stewing meat. It is still so used in dialects throughout England. The shift in meaning to a frying pan took place only in America, but an advertisement of 1790, offering for sale "bakepans, spiders, skillets," would suggest that even as late as this a distinction between the two was recognized.

The examples above have been offered only as a suggestion of the various language processes which have played a part in the distribution and meaning of some of our dialect terms. It is quite obvious that no definite conclusions about such matters can be reached on the basis of rather scant linguistic details. Such evidence as has been accumulated, however, seems to suggest that Kurath's original intuition was correct in that only home and farm terms give much evidence of regional or local distribution in the United States.

The question of social dialects or speech differences is quite another matter, with many scholars seeing much more profound grammatical differences between social—especially ethnic—groups. Black English, of which Gullah is the extreme case, comes immediately to mind; but the English of the Pennsylvania Germans also offers some grammatical constructions that are very strange to mainstream American English speakers.

Frequently, the matter of social dialect has been conceptualized in terms of "standard" and "nonstandard" dialects. H. L. Mencken believed in a so-called "American Vulgate" with reasonably uniform characteristics throughout the country—and with no special stated social distribution. Nonstandard dialects, however, do have many features in common, for whatever reason that may be.

One of the inflectional forms most characteristic of nouns in nonstandard American English is the unchanged plural after numbers: *six mile down the road, five foot tall,* and similarly applied to *month, year,* and *gallon.* In Black English it resembles the Afro-Creole non-redundant pluralization: *The boys* bears a plural inflection, but either *six boy* or *plenty boy* is plural without the final *s.* Any plural marking in the immediate environment, not just a numeral, may suffice, so that we sometimes find sentences like *Dem chair* for "Those are chairs."

The Mencken-type Vulgate may, in the case of some unmarked plurals, represent a preservation of linguistically older forms than those found in Standard English. It displays the opposite tendency, however, in the possessive pronoun in its so-called absolute form, which in the standard language represents a strange and inconsistent mixture of patterns. *Mine* and the archaic *thine* are derived from the adjectival form by adding *-n*. *Hers, ours, yours,* and *theirs,* on the other hand, add *-s* to the adjectival form. *His* and *its* are indistinguishable so far as their secondary and absolute forms are concerned. In contrast, the "Vulgate" possessive pronouns, *mine, yourn, hisn, hern, ourn, theirn,* present a perfectly regular pattern formed by an analogical extension of *mine* and *thine* to the third person singular and to the plural forms. The fact that Pidgin English probably had absolute *me one, you one, he one,* etc., may have contributed something to the leveling process of the Vulgate.

In the use of absolute possessives, Black English and other non-standard dialects part company. In the most extreme form, which William Stewart calls *basilect,* Black English has *he book, you friend, they uncle.* In the "exposed" position, *It he book* becomes neither *It he* nor *It hisn.* Instead, basilect *It he own* alternates with a Standard-English influenced *It his.*

The reflexive pronouns give us another instance of a more regular operation of analogy on the nonstandard level than on the standard. In Standard English, *myself, yourself, ourselves,* and *yourselves* are combinations of the genitive pronoun plus the singular or plural of the *-self* form; *himself* and *themselves* employ the object form of the pronoun, whereas *herself* and *itself* could be either. Nonstandard English, in substituting *hisself* and *theirself* in the third person and adhering to the singular of *self* in *ourself* and *yourself* (plural), is not only more consistent but more economical in that the latter combinations signal the plural only once and avoid the redundancy of the plural *-selves.* The only ambiguity is in the second person, but the second personal pronoun has lost its distinctions between singular and plural anyway, except for non-standard formations like the Southern *you all*—which never figures in the reflexive.

One curious feature of the nonstandard pronoun is the substitution of the object for the subjective form in such sentences as *Us*

girls went home, John and her was married, Me and him was late.
The use of the object form for the subject is normal in Black English basilect (*Me help you?*) and in Pidgin English. In Cajun English, of Louisiana, it can be used at the end of the sentence for emphasis: *I was late, me.* In the "Vulgate," however, it seems to occur principally when the subject is compound or when the pronoun is syntactically a modifier of the subject, as in *us girls* above. The schools have made such emphatic use of *we girls* and *It is I* (or *he, she*), that the result is a lot of overcorrection on the order of *between you and I* (or even *between he and I*); *She gave it to Mother and I; She took all of we children.*

A few typical nonstandard inflectional forms deserve mention. *Them* as a demonstrative adjective (*them books*) probably harks back to the days when the English article and the demonstrative *that* (dative ðæm) were one and the same form. *Dem* is the regular demonstrative adjective and noun pluralizer (*dem man* = "men") in Gullah, but postposed use as in Jamaican and other creoles (*man-dem*) is hinted at in the records of early Black English in one speech by newly imported African slaves and remembered by Frederick Douglass. The multiple negative was a regular and accepted feature of older English, but Black English negative concord (*It ain't no cat can't get in no coop*) has no such obvious earlier parallel. The adverb without the -*ly* suffix or other differentiation from the adjective (*He spoke quiet; You did real good*) may reflect very old practices in English.

The standard and nonstandard languages are undoubtedly farthest apart with regard to verb forms. Black English non-passive preverbal *been* (*He been rub me the wrong way*), and *be* in its negation by *don't,* and in contrast to "zero copula" are the most extremely different forms outside Gullah *de.* Less significantly, there is a tendency to dispose of the distinctive -*s* inflection for the third person singular, either by eliminating it in such forms as *he want, she write,* etc., or by extending the peculiar form of the third person to the first and second—*I has some good friends; You is in lots of trouble.* Black English makes widespread, often hyper-corrective, use of these forms; the records tend to indicate that older varieties used (also hypercorrectively) *he am,* etc.

The overwhelming tendency in English verb development throughout the last seven or eight centuries has been toward an aggrandizement of the regular or weak inflection (*-ed* past tense) at the expense of the older minor conjugations. This is in effect a tendency toward a two-part verb, the infinitive or present stem opposed to an identical past tense and past participle. In general, this has been brought about through analogical processes. It is often impossible to know for certain whether nonstandard forms are the result of retention of an older preterite plural (*writ* as the past tense of *write;* or *begun* and *swum* in that function), or of analogies which have not operated in Standard English. Extension of the regular past inflections to such irregular verbs as *know* and *see* (*knowed, seed*) can only be analogical; as must the amalgamation of the strong preterite or past participle with the complementary form (*I taken, he done* as preterites; *have gave, have wrote, has went* as past participial forms).

The easy transition from one social class to another in the United States has resulted in a very hazy line of demarcation between what is acceptable and what is considered illiterate. According to the most rigorous textbook standard, some of the language employed in American legislative councils and in business life would not pass muster; one could not even be sure that what is spoken in college faculty meetings would always meet those same criteria. The awareness of this, combined with an unrealistic treatment of language in our schools, has resulted at times in a defiance of these questionable standards, in what could be called "dramatic low status assertion." More often it has given people guilt complexes about the language they use. The puristic school-teacher for whom nothing is good enough, has been attacked in linguistics courses and textbooks since the 1940's. Some changes may have been made, but the prescriptive attitude, in one guise or another, lives on in our school systems and in handbooks of usage. On television's Public Broadcasting System, groups consisting of actors, drama critics, newscasters, and occasionally even a linguistics professor meet to discuss the "deplorable" state of the English language in America.

Consequently, many Americans, especially those who are socially mobile, lack confidence and assurance of the essential aptness and correctness of their speech. Fewer members of any class are able to switch comfortably between a non-standard dialect and the standard—although this is by no means rare in other countries. Those educational programs that have called for use of children's home and peer group dialects in such educational activities as initial or remedial reading have generally met with scorn, even from many dialectologists. The Ann Arbor, Michigan, school district became in July, 1979, the first U.S. school system ordered to take Black children's dialect into account in planning its curriculum. Lawsuits similar to the one that elicited this decision have already been filed in Tampa, Florida, and Houston, Texas, and many others may follow.

Within professional dialectology, new developments like variation theory and inherent variability provide an even more solid foundation for acceptance of and interest in dialect and speech pattern differences. Popularization of the variable rule may be more difficult to achieve than was the case of regional and local differences; but there also seems to be less chance that the popularized knowledge will form the basis for invidious comparisons and linguistic snobbery. There is still some faith in the notion that understanding is the key to tolerance.

8
The Names Thereof

The moment we move out of our accustomed environment we are assailed by a host of unfamiliar names. Most visitors to the nation's capital cannot fail to be aware of the alphabetical designations for a host of streets and the use of the names of states for avenues. The New England family names on the mail boxes of rural Vermont make their impact upon the visitor at least as strongly. The traveler in West Africa is amazed and delighted by names for "Mammy Wagons" like *People Will Talk of You, Amen,* and *Always on Top* (the last being somewhat inappropriately in a ditch); and the visitor to the West Indies finds very similar names like *Sand in My Shoes, Lover's Prayer, Let Them Say,* and *Mi Kon Fo Doe* (Sranan Tongo for "I Came to Do") on carts and buses. In a similar manner, the totality of naming practices in America produces a powerful effect upon the newcomer to our shores, just as those of France, Germany, or even England have an impact upon the American traveler.

It is scarcely necessary to demonstrate in detail that the problem of naming in the United States is vast and complex. The expanse of territory to be supplied with names is huge; the political subdivisions are almost innumerable when one considers the fifty states, each with anywhere from a dozen to more than a hundred counties, the subdivisions of the counties into townships or towns, the rivers, their tributaries, the lakes, the hills and mountains, the prairies and plains, to say nothing of the cities and villages. And of course, there are the people themselves, and here we encounter some quite different naming problems and practices, of which more will be said later. Let us begin with place designations.

In general the place-naming practices reflect those tendencies and influences which operated upon the American vocabulary as a whole. Just as the colonists came to the shores of this country speaking language varieties current at the time, so had they brought with them a host of names for places familiar to them in their own country, which they immediately applied to their newly created settlements. Particularly in New England does one find perpetuated the names common to the English countryside. Bath in Maine; Brentwood and Croydon in New Hampshire; Danby and Maidstone in Vermont; Andover, Leominster, and Salisbury in Massachusetts; Colchester and Norwich in Connecticut; and Exeter in Rhode Island are only a few instances, typical of dozens of others.

Even before the arrival of the permanent settlers, the explorers and, in part, the monarchs who financed and promoted the expeditions exercised some control over the names which were conferred upon vast stretches of unexplored territory and the bodies of water adjacent to them. Many of these names were commemorative. Cape Anne was named in honor of the mother of King Charles. Cape Elizabeth, Cape James, Cape Henry are all self-explanatory, as indeed are Virginia, the Carolinas, Maryland, and Georgia, each of the last-named reflecting a different monarchical period of discovery and settlement. Moreover, as settlement spread westward, many of the traditional English names were reapplied to newly established places on the frontier. We know, for example, that Boston, Massachusetts, was named for the city in Lincolnshire, but it is more than likely that those in Alabama,

Indiana, Kentucky, Missouri, New York, Ohio, Pennsylvania, Tennessee, Texas, and possibly the one in Georgia, derived their name from the already existing Massachusetts settlement.

The kind of name transference that has just been described strikes one as a highly conscious process compared with the almost casual way in which place names seem to have developed in England and Western Europe. Of course there the place names reflect centuries of historical and cultural development, to say nothing of changes in languages as well. But nowhere in the many excellent and detailed investigations into the place names of Germany, France, and England does one sense the urgency of naming on a large scale, nor is he likely to encounter for these countries many specific statements of the reasons why one or another name was finally—and consciously—agreed upon. In this connection, George R. Stewart, in *Names on the Land,* cites two passages which are very revealing. The first of these, by a Puritan Chronicler, sets forth the basis of the commemorative practice in these terms:

> Why they called it Dorchester [Massachusetts] I never heard; but there was some of Dorsetshire and some of ye town of Dorchester that settled there, and it is very likely it might be in honor of ye aforesaid Revd. Mr. White of Dorchester.

The second is a Connecticut court resolution of 1658, which broadens this into a general principle:

> Whereas, it hath been a commendable practice of the inhabitants of all the Colonies of these parts, that as this Country hath its denomination from our dear native Country of England, and thence is called New England, so the planters, in their first settling of most new plantations have given names to those plantations of some Cities and Towns in England, thereby intending to keep up and leave to posterity the memorial of several places of note there, as Boston, Hartford, Windsor, York, Ipswich, Braintree, Exeter.

Also, the concluding portion of this name resolution points to a development which was to occur over and over again in the course of the settlement of the country:

> Considering that there is yet no place in any of the colonies
> that has been named in memory of the City of London, there
> being a new plantation within this Jurisdiction of Connecti-
> cut settled upon the fair River of Monhegin, in the Pequot
> Country, it being an excellent harbor and a fit and convenient
> place for future trade, it being also the only place which the
> English of these parts have possessed by conquest, and that
> by a very just war upon that great and warlike people the
> Pequots, that therefore they might thereby leave to posterity
> the memory of the renowned city of London, from whence
> we had our transportation, have thought fit, in honor to that
> famous City, to call the said plantation, New London.

Not only was New London born of this reasoning, but also the innumerable combinations with *New* which dot the country from
coast to coast. In addition to the ten Bostons in states other than
Massachusetts, we must also reckon with eight New Bostons.
Four New Baltimores, five New Bedfords, an even dozen New
Londons, and six New Richmonds serve to give some idea of the
prevalence of this combination in a country that for three centuries considered itself new, wholly or in part.

Just as the American vocabulary as a whole added elements of
the various non-English cultures which the colonists encountered,
so do the place names reflect these same linguistic contacts, often
more extensively than the vocabulary as a whole—but often, like
the general vocabulary, with secondary influences. This is particularly true of the American Indian language influence: from one
part of the country to another, from Walla Walla to Waxahachie,
from Kissimmee to Kalamazoo, our map is dotted with all kinds
of Indian names. They are on the lips of our people every day.
They constitute an integral part of the flavor of American life and
culture. Even the names of twenty-seven of the fifty states of the
Union could be said to be, more or less, of Indian origin. (There
has been considerable debate about the exact nature of some of
these, especially Idaho.)

But, as with the general vocabulary, the precise tally of these
names is complicated. What Kelsie Harder calls "linguistic inter-
facing" occurred—the sometimes abrasive rubbing together of lan-

guages. He cites the example of Bogalusa, Louisiana, which has been rendered in Spanish, English, French, and American folk spellings: Arroyo Negro o Bos-holizà; Black Creek; Bogue Luca; Bogue Loosa; and Bogue Lusa. An occasional name like Hatchie River (Mississippi—Tennessee) combines an English and an Indian (here, Choctaw) word for the same meaning. The assessment of Indian language influence is far from an automatic process, especially where Baton Rouge represents a translation from Choctaw *istroum* ("red post"), or where Choctaw *Uski Chitto* ("Big Cane"), has become Whiskey Chitto by folk etymology.

These place names represent, then, various types of linguistic treatment. Often the English-speaking settlers merely took over, more or less accurately, the name given to a place by the Indians themselves. Frequently such names were descriptive of the landscape or of the life about it. Mackinac Island has already been explained as a shortening of *Michilimackinac,* "great turtle." *Mississippi* is simply "big river." (Examples of English *big,* Indian language etymons like Choctaw *chitto,* French *grand,* and Spanish *grande* all add up to an impressive number of place names where attention is paid to the element of largeness.) The name *Chicago* has several interpretations, the most likely being "garlic field," with the final *-o* serving really as a locative suffix. Occasionally Indian names were given to places by white settlers who were familiar with one or another of the various Indian languages. This was the case with Negaunee "high place" in Michigan, named by Peter White, and a number of Michigan counties have Indian names coined by Henry Rowe Schoolcraft. In fact Schoolcraft, an assiduous collector of Indian lore—Longfellow based his *Hiawatha* on Schoolcraft's work—let his enthusiasm for Algonquian names run away with him to such a degree that the Michigan legislature finally revolted against such unpronounceable specimens as Kaykakee, Mikenauk, Notipekago, Aishcum, and Cheonoquet, and substituted a number of simple Irish names like Clare, Emmet, and Roscommon for those which the expert had devised.

Many times in the course of our name giving, the Indian name was translated into its English equivalent. As the survey of place names in South Dakota puts it, "When a creek is called White Thunder, Blue Dog, or American Horse, the Indian influence is obvious, since these adjectives are not those which a white man would ordinarily use with these nouns. Four Horns, Greasy Horn, and Dog Ear are other examples." The survey neglected to mention Stinking Water and Stinking Bear creeks, both of which are further convincing and delightful illustrations of this same process.

Finally, American Indian tribal or personal names are often applied to places. To quote again from George R. Stewart's *Names on the Land,* "Famous chiefs were admired as good warriors or defenders of the liberty of their people. Powhatan, Tecumseh, Pontiac . . . became names of towns and counties. Even the grotesque Cornplanter appeared as a Pennsylvania town. Osceola, a Florida Seminole, gave his name to seventeen places in far-scattered states." Similarly, such names as Genesee, Muskingum, Miami, Huron, and Narragansett all perpetuate the names of Indian nations.

In the New York area many place names have remained as a testimony to the original Dutch settlement. Many of these were imported directly from Holland, among which may be included Harlem, Staten (Island), Flushing (Dutch *Vlissingen*), Yonkers, and Spuyten Duyvil. In addition, we took from the Dutch a large number of compounding place-name elements such as -*dorp*, -*kill* for "channel," -*hook*, and -*clove* for "ravine." Sometimes these combined with Dutch elements, at other times with English, as can be seen in formations like Sandy Hook, Kinderhook, Peekskill, Catskill, Schuylkill, New Dorp, North Clove, and the tautological formation Clove Valley. Later areas of Dutch settlement appear to have employed only such direct borrowings as Vriesland, Zealand, Drenthe, Overisel, and Graafschap, all in Michigan, and these only for town names. In Michigan and Iowa the Dutch naming influence did not extend to features of the topography.

A well-defined sector of place names in the United States gives evidence of the originally French colonial status of a considerable portion of the country. These names fall into two broad classes: such descriptive terms as Detroit, Au Sable, Ecorse, Grand Blanc, Eau Claire, Prairie du Chien, Fond du Lac; and commemorative names like Louisiana, La Salle, Charlevoix, Marquette, Lafayette, St. Ignace, and St. Joseph. The descriptive terms were often given by the French themselves, or at times were actually translations of earlier Indian place names, as for example Platte River (originally Rivière Plate), an attempt to render Choctaw *ni*, "river," and *bthaska*, "spreading flatness."

Two other place-naming practices stemming from French influence should be mentioned. Hundreds of towns and cities all over the United States have the French suffix *-ville* as part of their name (Nashville, Louisville, Jacksonville, etc.), a feature which is certainly not common in England. The *-ville* craze, resulting at times in such bizarre formations as Applebachsville, appears to have begun late in the eighteenth century and to have attained startling proportions early in the nineteenth. Matthew Arnold's comment on this practice is worth quoting: "What people in whom the sense of beauty and fitness was quick [i.e., alive] could have invented or could tolerate the hideous names ending in *ville*, the Briggsvilles, Higginsvilles, Jacksonvilles, rife from Maine to Florida; the jumble of unnatural and inappropriate names everywhere?"

Less obvious but of equal importance is the word order in such names as Lake Superior and Lake Champlain where the general or common noun comes first and is followed, as in French, by the modifying or specific term. All the names of the Great Lakes follow this syntactical pattern, retaining their original order.

Place names of Spanish origin are centered chiefly in Florida and the Southwest. Their number has been estimated at over 2000. At least a fifth of those in California are saints' names—witness San Diego, Santa Monica, Santa Barbara, San Francisco—commemorating either the patron saint of the explorer who named the spot or the particular saint's day on which the discovery was made.

Some of the original Spanish names have since been translated:

Rio de los Santos Reyes has been displaced by the much more prosaic Kings River, and Rio de las Plumas by Feather River. In addition there may be found such hybrid combinations as Hermosa Beach and Point Loma, some of which, like the first, at least make sense, and others, like the second, betray the linguistic naïveté of the realtor who developed the subdivision and gave it its name.

One well-defined layer in the lexicon of American place names assumes far more prominence than in the vocabulary generally. These are names associated with classical antiquity. In a sense the tradition may be said to have begun with William Penn, who after his original suggestion of New Wales as a name for the land he was about to acquire in America was rejected by the King's secretary, proposed Sylvania as a second choice. The outcome, Pennsylvania, was placed in the charter by Charles II. Likewise the principal city of the new colony derived its name from classical sources, and almost every schoolboy in America knows that Philadelphia means "city of brotherly love."

A second impetus toward the adoption of Greek and Latin names came from a series of events occurring in the state of New York soon after the country gained its independence. First, a town meeting at Vanderheyden's Ferry in 1789 decided to rename that settlement Troy. Just a year later the Military Tract in the Finger Lakes area was divided into twenty-five townships; the commission entrusted with the disposal of public lands gave to all but three of these the name of a person celebrated in classical antiquity, ranging from Hector, Ulysses, and Romulus to Brutus and Cato, including the poets Virgil and Ovid. The original inspiration seems to have dried up at the end, permitting the inclusion of Locke, Milton, and Dryden, although these by no means detracted from the prevailing learned atmosphere. From these beginnings it was but a step to the establishment of a whole series of classical city names: again in New York we find a Carthage as well as a Rome, Ithaca, Corinth, and Syracuse, and even Ilion in addition to Troy.

As the New York settlers went on to the west, many of the classical names were transferred. The Ithacas in Michigan and Wisconsin, the Troys in Wisconsin and Iowa, can undoubtedly be explained on this basis, but actually something more than population movement and name transference is involved here. There was an awakening of interest in Greek and Roman antiquity throughout the country. Part of this can be explained by the development of secondary education; in dozens of academies the classical course, with Latin and Greek language, literature, history, and geography for its subject matter, was the accepted preparatory curriculum for college work. Also, as a consequence of our break from English political tradition, we tended in our first flush of republican enthusiasm to look to Rome as a model. Even architecturally the classical revival was sweeping the country, beginning first in the east but extending virtually to the Mississippi by the 1840's and 1850's, dotting the new towns and cities with courthouses built like Doric temples, homes with columned porticos, college buildings reproducing the detail of the Parthenon. The eleven Romes, nine Corinths, twelve Spartas, two Spartanburgs and the lone Spartansburg in the United States are indicative of but one aspect of a general cultural movement, which found a further outlet in the extension of -*sylvania* and -*opolis* as place-naming elements.

Another important layer of place names in America consists of those drawn from the Bible. The impulse of religious groups to emigrate as organized bodies seeking freedom of worship was so widespread from the very beginning of American colonization almost to the very end, it would have been strange indeed if the Bible had not been employed for the purpose of naming. Here it is interesting to observe that of the New England colonies, it is Connecticut rather than Massachusetts, despite the customary association of the latter with Puritanism, which has a well-defined sector of Biblical place names: Bethel, Bethlehem, Canaan, Gilead, Goshen, Hebron, Jordan, Lebanon, Mt. Carmel, and Sharon. George R. Stewart has suggested that these arose from the religious fervor accompanying the Great Awakening rather than from the earliest period of settlement.

The Moravians and the other minor sects from Middle Europe which came to settle in Pennsylvania, spread into New York and later moved southward as far as North Carolina and westward to Indiana and Iowa, were also responsible for a good many of the Bethels, Bethlehems, and Goshens, as well as Emmaus, Ephrata, and Nazareth. The Latter-day Saints left their mark upon the map of Utah with names like Moroni, Nephi, Lehi, and Alma, drawn from the Book of Mormon, and also with Zion, Moab, Paradise, and Eden from the Bible itself. In fact they almost succeeded in naming the state Deseret, a term for honey bee, also drawn from the Book of Mormon.

Nothing short of a volume could even begin to do justice to all the naming practices which came to be employed; space permits the mention of only one or two others. From the time of Roger Williams on, there was always a marked strain of Utopianism prominent in the settlement of America. Groups motivated by ideologies ranging all the way from socialism to vegetarianism (and sometimes including both) came from abroad or collected in this country, determined to establish new social orders. Frequently the ideals or aspirations of these groups were reflected by the names which they bestowed upon their newly founded communities. Thus there appear among our place names such abstractions as Providence, Concord, Hope, and Harmony. Another facet of this same naming practice is much more closely connected with the normal political development of the country and our early struggles for national existence. Places called Liberty, Union, Freedom, and Independence dot the length and breadth of the land, either in their simple forms or in such combinations as Uniontown and Libertyville.

How a single name can give rise to a brood of others is particularly well illustrated by an occurrence in southern Illinois. When settlers came to establish a new village at the junction of the Ohio and the Mississippi rivers, the general topography of the area suggested the site of the capital of Egypt; accordingly it was called Cairo. As other villages came into being, the pattern was extended, and we find Karnak, Thebes, and Joppa. Finally the whole area became known as Egypt, a name which has persisted well over a century although it is not recorded on the maps. For a time there was even a distinction between Little Egypt, the territory immediately surrounding Cairo, and Greater Egypt, applied to a somewhat more extended area.

Thus far our principal concern has been the importation of place names. Nevertheless all the other linguistic processes which contributed to the development of the American vocabulary as a whole are reflected in our place-naming processes, very often in connection with the common nouns, the toponymic designations which enter into place-name combinations. For example, the American as well as the general English colonial use of *creek* reflects a change of meaning from "inlet" to "stream tributary." The reason was probably that waterways originally designated "creeks," when more fully explored, were often found to be tributaries of greater length.

Today, *creek* is probably the most common American term for something smaller than a river, often tributary to it, but its application in various parts of the country depends in part at least upon the nature, size, and extent of the surrounding network of waterways. Many a creek in Ohio would be called a river in the neighboring state of Michigan. *Creek* has entered into hundreds if not thousands of place-name combinations throughout the country.

Instances of transference from British regional or dialect use are to be found in *run,* also a term for a small stream, and *swamp,* the common American designation for marshy or boggy land. The former appears to have been originally Scottish or northern English; even its first citation in the literary language is to be found in the works of Boswell. This is more than a century later than its appearance in America, where it was used by early settlers and explorers in Massachusetts and Virginia. *Swamp* is recorded late in the seventeenth century as a south and east country word, and *sump* with this meaning is to be found in the north. In America the earliest recorded examples of the term occur with reference to

Virginia, but it spread very rapidly to all parts of the eastern coast.

Gulch, chiefly a western American term for a ravine, canyon, or gully, also has its origins in the English dialect vocabulary, but this time with functional change; its probable origin was a verb *gulch* or *gulsh,* "to sink in." *Bluff* for a steep river bank or shore is likewise the product of a transference of grammatical function. It was used first as an adjective, applied originally to ships that presented a broad flattened front and then to a shore or coastline of the same general contour, especially in the combinations *bluff land* and *bluff point.* Finally in South Carolina and Georgia the nouns were simply omitted, the adjective thus acquiring substantive use.

In short, toponymy is one of the divisions of the lexicon where sharp differences have developed between American and British English. Words like *fen, heath, moor,* and *coomb,* to mention only a few, common in England, invariably have a literary flavor for the American because he encounters them only in books. They are not part of his everyday vocabulary. The topography of America was just different enough from that of the mother country to favor the development of an indigenous set of toponyms, which in turn occur over and over again in our place names.

Word blending too has had a very specific role in the development of our place names, particularly in connection with cities and villages situated across our state borders and to a lesser extent our national boundaries. Texarkana is probably the best known of these, but there are also Kenova (Kentucky, Ohio, West Virginia), Calneva, Calvada, Calada, Calzona, Calexico (all pertaining to California and its adjacent states), and Delmarva (Delaware, Maryland, Virginia). According to George R. Stewart, some sixty names of this type mark the lines between various Southern and Far Western states. Upon occasion the blending process in place names operates in a somewhat more cryptic fashion. Marenisco, Michigan, was formed from the first syllables of the names of the first woman settler, Mary Relief Niles Scott, and according to one story at least, Azusa, California, grows everything from A to Z in the USA.

American street names also tend to reflect subconscious cultural tendencies. Our cities did not grow by gradual extension or accretion as did their European counterparts; usually they were laid out or plotted in advance of settlement. At the very least this necessitated the naming of many streets at a single time, often permitting a process of free association to operate. More commonly, street names were assigned on the basis of some ordered scheme.

As early as the seventeenth century, when Philadelphia was plotted, the streets running in one direction were simply numbered. Those cutting them at right angles were named—or at least many of them—after the various trees which grew there. In so doing Penn originated a system the essential elements of which were to be followed in city after city in the new continent. These elements are, first of all, a four-square or rectangular plan, with streets running at right angles to each other; second the frequent use of numbers for the one tier or series of streets, often reaching into the hundreds, as in present-day New York and Chicago; third, a varied but nonetheless systematic scheme for naming the second series of streets. The use of letters of the alphabet in Washington, D.C., has already been mentioned. Often a row of streets will be named after the Presidents of the United States in successive order; many a city has at least the vestigial remnants of such a system, with Washington Street somewhere near the center of business, followed by Adams, Jefferson, and so on, the name of the last president in the series indicating just about the time that portion of the city was plotted. In one section of Denver, Colorado, the streets were given Indian tribal names arranged in alphabetical order, from Acoma and Bannock to Yuma and Zuni. A second series honored famous Americans, also in alphabetical order beginning with Alcott and Bryant; a third perpetuates the names of United States senators, a fourth the justices of the Supreme Court. Whatever scheme or system is followed is irrelevant; the point is that such a system exists. Still another kind of schematization is to be found in the distinction between the term *street* for thoroughfares running in one direction and *avenue* for those at right angles to them, the plan followed in the portion of Manhattan which was plotted early in the nineteenth century.

We must remember, too, that this is a continuing process; as subdivisions are added to cities, the problems must be faced again and again. Any collection of names may be drawn upon for the purpose. One portion of Los Angeles is heavily indebted to the novels of Sir Walter Scott. State capitals sometimes use the names of the counties in that state, a practice suggested by the application of state names to the diagonal avenues in Washington, D.C. Small-town subdivisions tend to have ludicrously pretentious names like Sherwood Forest or International Estates. The latter, from Grand Prairie, Texas, has streets with names like Austrian, Canadian, British, and Swiss.

There is also Main Street, that most typically American designation for the principal thoroughfare, which attained such prominence as the title of Sinclair Lewis's popular and important novel that in many ways it has become a symbol of small-town life. In England the principal street is often called High, the adjective denoting importance rather than elevation, just as it is used there in *high road* and *highway*. There are some High Streets in the older cities along the eastern seaboard of the United States, but apparently as settlement moved inward into hillier country, *high* came to suggest physical elevation. Consequently the principal street in a village was spoken of as "the main street," and eventually this became petrified into a proper name. As early as 1687 a Pennsylvania record was entitled, "A late Order for ye Viewing and Discussing a maine Road from ye Center of Philadelphia ye Shortest way to ye falls." Most American cities bordering or spanning a river have a Front Street; a Market Street is to be found in many business sections.

Another feature of American street naming is the variety of substitute terms for the word *street*. The use of *avenue* has already been mentioned. *Court,* which in England usually refers to a confined yard on more or less quadrangular space opening off a street and built around with houses, is frequently used in the United

States for a short street, not more than one or two blocks in length. *Boulevard,* scarcely used in England at all, is applied in America to an exceptionally broad street or main traffic artery (e.g., Wilshire Boulevard in Los Angeles), and in some parts of the country refers specifically to streets which reserve a strip at the center for shade trees. Recently American city planners have tended to give up the four-square plan for residential districts, particularly those designed for larger dwellings, in favor of winding and even circular streets, thus affording variety of contour and often more lawn space. As a result a number of new names have come into use, among them *drive, crescent, circle,* and *parkway. Road* is also employed, presumably for its suggestion of the suburban. It is thus becoming a mark of distinction in some quarters to live on something other than a street or avenue.

There are, however, certain street-naming practices current in some parts of the world which have not established a foothold in the United States. Except for using the names of our chief executives and lawmakers on both the state and national level and an occasional name like Constitution Avenue, we have kept politics pretty well out of our street names. A Paseo de la Reforma is quite unlikely here; we have no Boulevards of the Declaration of Independence or Avenues of the Emancipation Proclamation. Nor do we memorialize the days or dates important in our national history by attaching them to streets, as is so often done in Latin America: Fifth of May in Mexico and Tenth of August in Ecuador. And certainly there is a foreign and somewhat artificial ring to *Avenue of the Americas,* the name given to Sixth Avenue in New York in the atmosphere of post-World War II internationalism. Old-time New Yorkers still call it Sixth Avenue anyway.

Moreover, our street names have the quality of permanence; when they are changed, it is principally to avoid possible confusion arising from similarity or duplication. We seldom rename principal streets after the heroes of the moment; and since our political life is stable, there is no call for a rapid succession of names assigned to commemorate the current national leader.

For a country of more than 200 million inhabitants whose ancestors came from all parts of the world, a systematic treatment of personal names would be even more complex than one dealing with place names or with the vocabulary in general. All that can be done here is to mention some of the principal tendencies and attitudes which prevail today.

First, some brief observations about given names are in order. Despite the strong Puritan influence in the northern colonies, the most absurd excesses of Puritan naming practices are somewhat less apparent in New England than in the mother country. True enough, names like Increase and Preserved are to be found among our early settlers, but one rarely encounters such monstrosities as Search-the-Scriptures or Hate-Evil. However, their other practice, that of adopting Old Testament names, often those which were harsh and unpleasant, persisted well into the nineteenth century. Today the Abimelechs, Eliphalets, Zachariahs, and Hezekiahs have virtually disappeared.

As far as the surnames are concerned, the principal force which has affected them is the pressure for conformity. This is not to say, of course, that foreign surnames do not persist in America. They do, and often to a surprising degree. The country was not very old before it had a Van Buren as president, and any list of names drawn at random today—a sampling of Who's Who, the members of Congress, an army promotion calendar—will show a wider diversity of national origin than one is likely to encounter almost anywhere in the world. However, there are often as many concealed or converted foreign names as those which are obviously and openly so.

To begin with, there are names which have been respelled, either out of deference to general English orthographic practice or because our alphabet lacks the necessary characters and diacritics. We have no wedges for c's and s's; thus a Slavic Jakša often becomes Jackson. The lack of umlaut sign converts a German Müller into either Miller or Muller, with Mueller as an outside possibility. König becomes either Konig or Koenig, or is translated into King.

Since surnames in many languages represent a patronymic compound (son of someone or other) spelled solidly, they are likely to be long and awkward-looking. In American practice these are often clipped, so that Tomaszewski becomes Thomas, Szymanowski is changed into Simon, and Pappadimitricopoulos emerges as Pappas. Upon occasion such a patronymic as Ivanovich is simply translated into its English equivalent, Johnson.

The longer a national group has been in the country, the greater the process of assimilation to English pronunciation patterns is likely to be. Thus French Langlois is scarcely to be recognized in Langley, St. Cyr in Sears, or German Huber in Hoover. Snyder is in a sense a respelling of Schneider, but it also demonstrates the restricted occurrence of an initial *shn-* cluster in English. Sounds which do not occur in English at all are either approximated or reconstituted, sometimes in ways which on the surface appear to be quite inexplicable. German Bach is often pronounced with the vowel of *law* and no final consonant at all and may be respelled as Baugh—or Steinbach as Stinebaugh.

In addition to respelling and phonetic approximation, translation provides the other principal means of assimilating foreign names. As early as the eighteenth century there is evidence of German Zimmermann, Jäger, Braunfeld, and Grünbaum appearing as Carpenter, Hunter, Brownfield, and Greentree. The process has continued with other national or linguistic groups—witness the large numbers of persons of Finnish extraction named Lake and Hill, translations of Järvinen and Maki, possibly the two most common Finnish surnames.

Not all foreign names suffer a status loss in translation. Dutch names, particularly those associated with the Hudson Valley and old New York, have acquired not merely general acceptance but indeed an aura of respectability. *Knickerbocker* retains some function as a symbol of New York City, and it seems especially significant that the city's professional basketball team is named the Knicks (New York Knickerbockers). Value extends as well to French and Spanish surnames in those parts of the country where those nationalities were among the earliest settlers.

Many special naming problems are so complex that they can only be mentioned. No onomastic problem is greater than that of the American Negroes, who after Emancipation had to provide themselves with permanent surnames. West African naming practices were so successfully masked that many an alleged authority asserted, with full confidence, that no such practices survived even in the fairly early slave populations. The general American public got its first exposure to such survivals in Alex Haley's televised novel *Roots,* in which Kunta Kinte strove to maintain his name and identity by resisting the slave name Toby. Famous athletes have taken Moslem names like Muhammad Ali and Kareem Abdul-Jabbar, but perhaps the most pervasive survival is the very widespread use of often exotic nicknames. The West African practice of giving day names—seven male and seven female—for the day of the week on which children were born (*Cuffee* for males born on Friday, *Cudjo* for those born on Monday) survived in forms similar to the original and in translation. Lorenzo Dow Turner's *Africanisms in the Gullah Dialect* (1949), found great numbers of African survivals in Sea Island naming practices, and more recent research has found somewhat reduced traces of the same processes throughout the United States. There are even less modified African naming practices extant in the West Indian islands.

There are many other groups with distinctive naming patterns. Hawaiians are an obvious example, and even some *haoles* who grew up on the islands took a third name like *Kamehameha* to go with the conventional American first and middle names. Jewish naming influences are perhaps even subtler, as survivals, than those of Blacks; Yehudi and Moshe clearly reflect Hebrew religious feeling, but the custom of naming a child with a word allit-

erative to that of a revered ancestor makes even Morris and Milton Jewish in everything but etymology. Many a girl of Jewish
descent is Sarah to her family and Sandra to the outside world.
The relatively small numbers of genuine Gypsies in the United
States (often confused with unrelated groups sharing similar life
styles) frequently have two such sets of names.

A competent study of personal naming practices in the United
States would have as its first requisite a detailed understanding of
the complex psychology, the ambitions, hopes, and aspirations as
well as the taboos of each of the immigrant groups arriving on our
shores. Such a study would have to look beneath the official
veneer of conformity to the mainstream in order to search out the
ways in which minority groups maintain an almost clandestine
pattern of identity; one not often recognized or recognizable by
any group other than themselves.

9

American English, International English, and the Future

The development of American English, and the relationship of this development to the most salient features in the cultural life and history of the American people, has been the primary concern of the preceding chapters. Socio-political factors such as the expression of American military might during and after World War II, the extension of American influence in East Asia, and recent developments in the Middle East, have all contributed to the establishment of English as the unofficial second language of almost the entire world. The propagation of English as a second language gained even greater momentum through the efforts of the Fulbright Commission, the United States Information Agency, and the Peace Corps, as well as other State Department and governmental agencies. America's industry and commerce; its post-World War II emergence as a technological leader; and the world-wide network of communication which is now an established fact of modern life, have all combined to insure that in almost any corner of the earth, at any time of day, English is in use.

It was during this same period that the whole methodology of English language teaching became an important issue. It has been argued, rather unconvincingly, that English is an "easy language to learn" and that it is "natural" for such widespread use to develop. It has been claimed that the comparative freedom of modern English from inflectional endings—as compared to Russian or German—makes it potentially the international language. It has also been pointed out that much of its vocabulary is composed of words both of Latin and Teutonic origin, making large portions of its word stock readily comprehensible to millions of speakers of other languages.

Vocabulary borrowings have been especially heavy, so that languages like Spanish have come to acquire baseball terminology (for example, *siore* "shortstop"), and Swahili to have automobile terminology (*gear*) as part of their everyday content. English forms many of its new technological terms (*polyester, astronaut*) from Greek etymons; whether independently of English or through its influence, many of the world's languages are using the same device. English *telephone* and German *Vernsprecher* were once greatly dissimilar, but the general German adoption of *Telephon* bridges the gap. Many comparable changes have taken place in the lexicons of the world's languages within the last three decades.

It can be argued, on much firmer grounds, that the Pidgin English which spread around the globe in the seventeenth, eighteenth, and nineteenth centuries—especially to islands and coastal areas—somehow accorded with "language universals" and was therefore easy to learn and retain. But Pidgin is in disrepute except in a few areas, and the English which bids fair to become the world's common language in the decade of the 1970's and 1980's is much nearer to what is usually called "standard" English.

Although some few may still ridicule an "American accent," there is little doubt that American is the variety of English most often heard abroad and therefore most imitated by second language learners. Most learners are not, however, especially interested in sounding "American." What they wish to master is general, or international, English.

At many times in the past, Americans have enjoyed the fiction that only non-native speakers could speak "perfect" English. This fiction was most frequently applied to Chinese and Japanese learners. The stereotypical portrayal of the movies' Charlie Chan, always played by an occidental, astonished unlettered native speakers with his ornate vocabulary. While this is clearly a fictional representation, it does have a small basis in truth. The English most easily learned by non-native speakers tends to be more formal in style and closer to the literary language than everyday American usage. Exceptions come primarily in the area of youth- and drug-culture users of Black or pseudo-Black slang. The January, 1973 issue of *Komunikason,* an underground publication in Papiamentu in Curaçao, called itself *Edishon di Freak-Out.* The same pattern may be repeated in places both more and less well-known.

English—excluding Pidgin and Creole varieties—increased from about 50 million speakers in 1600 to at least 280 million native speakers between 1600 and 1950. It might be argued that, if this fifty-five-fold multiplication were to be cut to merely a fivefold increase over the next four centuries, we might still expect one billion native speakers by 2350—nearly one-third of the present world population. The probability of such an increment is questionable, however, on the grounds that a feat similar to the opening up of the North American continent to settlers who eventually adopted the language is not likely to be duplicated.

It is in its development as a second language, however, that the current growth of English and its future development seem to lie. The various artificial international languages seem to have made little headway. Latin hardly exists as a Lingua Franca, and French, although very useful in places like Africa and the Near East, has gained no further ground in the twentieth century. In the Arabic countries and in places like Vietnam, where a generation ago every educated person would have known some French, English is now the second language most likely to have been acquired by this generation. In Mexico and parts of South America, Spanish is an important second language for American Indian language speakers.

In India, there were some politically motivated attempts to replace English, in its official language and language of wider communication functions, by one or another of the important indigenous languages. Advocates for Swahili can be found in East and Central Africa, where official trade between countries like Burundi and Kenya may be conducted in English, but covert activities are strictly in Swahili. Even in those areas, however, English is not without importance as a language of wider communication.

With British power almost completely gone and that of America threatened by the economic losses of the late 1970's, one may wonder how much longer English will hold onto its pre-eminent position. Is it so well established that, even if Americans no longer dominate the economic life of an area, the traders themselves will go on using it with everyone who does not speak their native language? Or will it disappear rapidly once no one feels the necessity of using English "so the Americans can understand"?

There is, at the present time, no certain way to answer those questions. It is well to keep in mind, however, the possibility that the military might of the Russians, or the sheer economic force of the newly rich Arabic nations, or the emergence of China as a world power may lead to a gradual replacement of English by one or more of those languages.

Whether or not everyone speaks English, it is very unlikely that the influence which English—and American English—has exerted over the languages of the world, particularly in vocabulary, will disappear any time soon. We know that, by about 1330, the Norman French spoken in England by the conquerors had become a much less important factor than it was 200 or even 100 years earlier, but we also know that the French borrowings of the period actually increased and have remained with us till the present day. We know that the use of Old Norse became unlikely in England in an even shorter time after the Viking invasions, but we also know that the borrowings from that language like *they, their,* and *them* and the verb *take,* which we got from the Norse in the Danelaw, have remained a permanent part of English. In like manner, no matter how learned Frenchmen may rail against "Franglais," Frenchmen are not likely to give up vocabulary like *zoning, by-pass, tanker, container,* or *hit parade* (although, if they follow American trends, they will replace the last by *top twenty* or *top forty*).

We can well expect, also, that English will continue its habit of picking up vocabulary from other languages. We know that dictionaries of English at various periods of its history seem to reflect consistent growth. Dictionaries of Old English, of the language as it was used approximately 975 years ago, contain about 37,000 words. A fairly complete dictionary of Middle English—that is, the language of 500 years ago—would have between 50,000 and 70,000 entries. It is likely that a dictionary of Early Modern English, the period of Shakespeare and his contemporaries, would contain at least 140,000 words, and unabridged dictionaries of present-day English have approximately half a million entries.

We also know that no one speaker at a given period of time uses anything approximating the complete vocabulary resources of the language. We are also beginning to appreciate the differential use of resources. A collection of idioms in Black English vernacular, for example, might include items like *love come down* (sexual desire was aroused), and *ace boon coon* (best friend). For a speaker of English as a second language, some special vocabulary is likely to remain a mystery, even though his English may be otherwise "perfect." So too will certain subtle distinctions remain obscure. Only a person who has lived in the United States for many years could be expected to know that the initial syllables of *Rockettes* and *rockabilly* are not the same etymon; one denotes *Rockefeller* Center and the other *rock* music.

There is, as suggested already, strong evidence for the conclusion that the English vocabulary is increasing. Even if we consider the possibility that the early records are so fragmentary that the numbers just cited for Old English and Middle English fall far short of what the language actually contained, still the apparent quadrupling of our stock of words during the last three and a half centuries is significant. The vocabulary increase, in turn, is indicative of increased cultural contacts. There is no reason to suppose that these contacts will not continue to increase—although perhaps not at the same rate. Some increase in the English vocabulary seems likely throughout the foreseeable future, especially if the English of the twentieth century continues to expand in international use.

We have noticed, also, that the recent extensions of our vocabulary have come not so much through word borrowing as from the manipulation of elements which are already in the language. Such processes as compounding, the addition of derivative prefixes and suffixes, change in grammatical function, and formation of new idioms account in great part for our recent changes. Without question we shall continue to borrow some words from foreign languages in the future. We did so during both world wars, and if the language continues to spread over areas of the Far East, for example, it is reasonable to look forward to new words coming from Malay, as well as from Russian, possibly even from Swahili and the Bantu languages. (Americans who have been stationed in East and Central Africa know at least *kabish* "very, extremely," and *kidogo* "a little.") But the principal growth in the English vocabulary will undoubtedly come as a result of the processes which have just been mentioned—up to what point is hard to guess. A doubling of the vocabulary in the next two centuries is not difficult to conceive of in light of what has happened since 1600.

But there will increasingly be the factor that many of the new words, compounds, and expressions will be understood only where there is more or less direct contact with the language(s) from which they are borrowed or where the activities and processes are actually going on. As present-day Americans, in general, know only a small portion of the 500,000 words in an unabridged dictionary, it is not unlikely that the restriction of future acquisitions to special groups should become an even greater factor. Anthony Burgess's novel *A Clockwork Orange,* which presents teenage-English so thoroughly infiltrated by Russian borrowings

(*devotchka* "girl," *malchik* "boy," *moloko* "milk," *Bog* "God")
that it is hardly intelligible to anyone who has not studied at least
some Russian, is exaggerated but, in principle, far from impossible.

The future possibility of further separation than now exists between varieties of English—at least the well-known British and
American varieties—seems even greater than in the past. Ability to
"speak English" will less and less guarantee perfect communication with others who use the same language, even fluently.
The use of more than one variety of English is now commonplace
in countries like Suriname and Sierra Leone. The development of
even more such situations is, at least theoretically, quite likely in
the future. If expansion goes on, prescriptive and puristic limitations on what is considered "English" will become increasingly
unrealistic and ultimately intolerable.

In short, international utility, not native speaker usage or pronunciation, may be the primary criterion for "good" English in
the future. Local and regional varieties, especially, can be expected
to diminish greatly in importance. What we know about change in
the past will, we hope, enable us to adjust more realistically to
what is sure to evolve in the future.

Appendix

Phonetic Alphabet

Vowels

ɑ	represents the sound of *a* in *father*.
æ	represents the sound of *a* in *mat*.
e	represents the sound of *a* in *fate*.
ε	represents the sound of *e* in *met*.
i	represents the sound of *ee* in *keep*.
I	represents the sound of *i* in *bit*.
ɔ	represents the sound of *au* in *autumn*.
o	represents the sound of *o* in *hope*.
u	represents the sound of *oo* in *food*.
U	represents the sound of *oo* in *good*.
ə	represents the sound of *a* in *above, Cuba*.

Consonants

b	represents the sound of *b* in *boy*.
d	represents the sound of *d* in *do*.

f   represents the sound of *f* in *first*.
g   represents the sound of *g* in *go*.
h   represents the sound of *h* in *hit*.
k   represents the sound of *k* in *cook*.
l   represents the sound of *l* in *let*.
m   represents the sound of *m* in *man*.
n   represents the sound of *n* in *no*.
ŋ   represents the sound of *ng* in *sing*.
p   represents the sound of *p* in *put*.
r   represents the sound of *r* in *robe*.
s   represents the sound of *s* in *soap*.
š   represents the sound of *sh* in *shell*.
t   represents the sound of *t* in *tie*.
θ   represents the sound of *th* in *thin*.
ð   represents the sound of *th* in *then*.
v   represents the sound of *v* in *very*.
w   represents the sound of *w* in *water*.
y   represents the sound of *y* in *yet*.
z   represents the sound of *s* in *rose*.
ž   represents the sound of *s* in *pleasure*.
č   represents the sound of *ch* in *cheese*.
ǰ   represents the sound of *g* in *gem*.

Diphthongs

aI   represents the sound of *ie* in *tie*.
aU   represents the sound of *ow* in *how*.
ɔI   represents the sound of *oy* in *boy*.

Bibliography

Allen, Harold and Underwood, Gary, eds. *Readings in American Dialectology.* New York: Appleton-Century-Crofts, 1971.

Blankenship, Russell. *American Literature as an Expression of the National Mind.* New York: Henry Holt and Company, 1931.

Bradford, William. *Of Plimmoth Plantation.* Boston: Wright and Potter Printing Company, 1898.

Dillard, J. L. *Black English.* New York: Random House, 1972.

———— *All-American English.* New York: Random House, 1975.

———— *Black Names.* The Hague: Mouton, 1975.

———— *Lexicon of Black English.* New York: Seabury Press, 1976.

Drechsel, Emanuel. *Mobilian Jargon: Linguistic, Sociocultural, and Historical Aspects of an American Indian Lingua Franca.* Dissertation, University of Wisconsin (Madison), 1979.

Foster, Brian. *The Changing English Language.* New York: St. Martin's Press, 1968.

Fox, George. Edited by John L. Nichalls. *The Journal of George Fox.* Cambridge: The University Press, 1952.

Harder, Kelsie. *Illustrated Dictionary of Place Names, United States and Canada.* New York: Van Nostrand Reinhold, 1976.

Krapp, George P. *The English Language in America.* New York: Century, 1925.

———— Revised by Albert H. Marckwardt. *Modern English, Its Growth and Use.* New York: Charles Scribner's Sons, 1969.

Kurath, Hans. *A Word Geography of the Eastern United States*. Ann Arbor: University of Michigan Press, 1949.

———— and McDavid, Raven I. *The Pronunciation of English in the Atlantic States*. Ann Arbor: University of Michigan Press, 1949.

Labov, William. *The Social Stratification of English in New York City*. Washington, D.C.: Center for Applied Linguistics, 1965.

Laird, Carlton. *Language in America*. New York: World Publishing Company, 1970.

Marryat, Captain Frederick. *Diary in America*. Edited by Jules Zanger. Indiana University Press, 1960.

Mencken, H. L. *The American Language*. First Edition. New York: Alfred A. Knopf, 1919.

———— *The American Language*. Second Edition. New York: Alfred A. Knopf, 1921.

———— *The American Language*. Third Edition. New York: Alfred A. Knopf, 1923.

———— *The American Language*. Fourth Edition. New York: Alfred A. Knopf, 1936.

———— *The American Language*. Supplement One. New York: Alfred A. Knopf, 1945.

———— *The American Language*. Supplement Two. New York: Alfred A. Knopf, 1948.

Mitford, Mary Russell. *Lights and Shadows of American Life*. London: H. Colburn and R. Bentley, 1832.

Nielson, Don and Nielson, Alleen Pace. *Language Play, An Introduction to Linguistics*. Rowley, Massachusetts: Newbury House, 1978.

O'Neil, Wayne. "The Politics of Bidialectalism." *College English*, XXIII (January, 1972): pp. 433–8.

Penn, William. *A Letter from William Penn, Proprietor and Governor of Pennsylvania in America, . . . Containing a General Description of Said Province, of the Natives or Aborigines*. London: A. Sowle, 1683.

Pickering, John. *Vocabulary, or Collection of Words and Phrases Which Have Been Supposed to Be Peculiar to the United States of America*. Boston: Cummings and Hilliard, 1816.

Pickford, Glenna Ruth. "American Linguistic Geography: A Sociological Appraisal." *Word*, 12 (1956): pp. 211–33.

Piozzi, Hester. *Anecdotes of the Late Samuel Johnson*. London: Cambridge University Press, 1789.

Pyles, Thomas. *Words and Ways in American English*. New York: Random House, 1952.

Read, William A. *Louisiana French*. Baton Rouge: LSU Press, 1963.

Rourke, Constance. *American Humor: A Study of the National Character*. New York: Harcourt, Brace, and Company, 1921.

Schele de Vere, Maximilian. *Americanisms: The English of the New World*. New York: Charles Scribner's Sons, 1872.

Steevens, George Warrington. *The Land of the Dollar*. New York: Dodd, Mead, and Company, 1897.

Stewart, George Rippey. *Names on the Land*. Boston: Houghton Mifflin, 1958.

—— *American Place-Names*. New York: Oxford University Press, 1970.

Stewart, William A. "Sociolinguistic Factors in the History of American Negro Dialects." *Florida FL Reporter,* 1967.

—— "Continuity and Change in American Negro Dialects." *Florida FL Reporter,* 1968.

Tucker, Gilbert M. *American English*. New York: Alfred A. Knopf, 1921.

Turner, Frederick Jackson. *The Frontier in American History*. New York: H. Holt and Company, 1920.

Turner, Lorenzo Dow. *Africanisms in the Gullah Dialect*. Chicago: University of Chicago Press, 1949.

Ward, Nathaniel. *The Simple Cobbler of Aggawan,* 1647. Reprinted in Boston for D. Henchman, 1713.

Wish, Harvey. *Society and Thought in America*. New York: Longmans Green, 1950.

Withers, Carl [pseudonym James West]. *Plainville, USA*. New York: Columbia University Press, 1945.

Zangwill, Israel. *The Melting Pot*. New York: The Macmillan Co., 1909.

Index